ZERO to HERO

Christine Wilding and Stephen Palmer

Hodder Arnold

A MEMBER OF THE HODDER HEADLINE GROUP

Cover © C Squared Studios/Photodisc/
Getty Images; Stockbyte/Getty Images
Illustrations by Barking Dog Art

Orders: Please contact Bookpoint Ltd, 130 Milton Park, Abingdon, Oxon OX14 4SB.
Telephone: (44) 01235 827720, Fax: (44) 01235 400454. Lines are open from 9.00 to 17.00, Monday
to Saturday, with a 24-hour message answering service. You can also order through our website
www.hoddereducation.com

British Library Cataloguing in Publication Data
A catalogue record for this title is available from the British Library.

ISBN-10 0340 915390
ISBN-13 9780 340915 394

First published   2006
Impression number   10 9 8 7 6 5 4 3 2 1
Year   2008   2007   2006

Typeset by Pantek Arts Ltd, Maidstone, Kent.
Printed in Great Britain for Hodder Arnold, a division of Hodder Headline,
338 Euston Road, London, NW1 3BH, by Bath Press, Bath.

Hodder Headline's policy is to use papers that are natural, renewable and recyclable products and made
from wood grown in sustainable forests. The logging and manufacturing processes are expected to
conform to the environmental regulations of the country of origin.

Every effort has been made to trace copyright for material used in this book. The authors and
publishers would be happy to make arrangements with any holder of copyright whom it has not been
possible to trace successfully by the time of going to press.

CONTENTS

CONTENTS

CONTENTS

DEDICATION

To everyone in my constantly expanding and delightful family, as well as special friends. With love and thanks to you all.

Christine

To Emma, Leah, Rebecca, Laura, Imogen, Liz, Joshua and Samuel. To our future generations.

Stephen

INTRODUCTION

As a coaching psychologist and a psychotherapist, we work on a daily basis with people who suffer from a lack of self-esteem. These people may present a variety of different problems to us, ranging from chronic depression to seeing their lives fall apart after a job loss, bereavement or other similar trauma. But one of the common threads running through this wide variety of problems is that these people can't deal successfully with these issues without professional help because of *their lack of confidence in their ability to do so.*

As therapists and as coaches, we're not there to resolve people's personal crises: we're there to build their self-esteem so that they can then resolve their own problems, however diverse and difficult these may be. It's these skills that we'd like to share with you in this book.

Of course, it doesn't always take a crisis or negative event to trigger low self-esteem. Some people feel that they've suffered in this way for most, if not all, of their lives. They may not even be aware of its existence, except in terms of their lack of belief that they can achieve what they want, that people will like them as they are, or that they deserve happiness and fulfilment in their lives.

The fact that you've taken the trouble to buy and start to read this book tells us that you think that you're suffering from low self-esteem, and that you'd seriously like to do something about it.

You've made a good decision! By the time you've worked through all the chapters of this book, *we're* confident that *you'll* feel confident. You'll understand the unhelpful thinking and self-defeating behaviour that leads us all down this path of thinking poorly about ourselves, and discover the confidence to live the life you want and achieve the goals you hope for.

The programme is organised into 100 days, or steps, and we're aware that this is a heavy workload, especially as each day is accompanied by a practical assignment for you to do. But the benefits will be worthwhile – think of yourself as taking 100 steps forward.

You can tackle an activity each day, or choose to pace yourself to take account of natural breaks that may occur in your learning. To keep up the momentum, you may find the daily approach provides the boost you need.

Each day of new learning is accompanied by an activity to keep you on your toes – and you have the option of signing up to extra tips and ideas sent to you via text messages. We'd encourage you to sign up to these. The texts will be the nearest thing to having us personally working alongside you at times when you might otherwise feel your confidence levels dipping.

The activities are the most important part of the book, and it's essential that you take them seriously. We'll never ask too much of you – sometimes they'll require you to do little more than ensure you really understand your learning for the day. *To help you fight low self-esteem we strongly suggest that you do the exercises.*

There's some further 'bad news' about the activities. They're not always 'one-offs'. Several of the points will be on-going. This is because you'll only internalise your new, more confident way of being by making your activities your new default. As you'll understand as you work on the exercises, we're also looking for patterns that are personal to you, and this kind of detective work only succeeds when you have a fair few samples to analyse.

The good news is that, as we emphasise in other parts of the book, nothing that we ask of you will take too long nor will it be too difficult (if you're intelligent enough to be reading this book, the tasks will be easy and fun!)

How to use this book

First, you need some tools

Do ensure that, before you start, you've bought two books – preferably hard-covered, A4 lined notebooks – get a whole handful of working roller-ball pens, and have a safe, quiet, personal place to keep them where they won't be pilfered by other members of the family or colleagues at work! Use hard-cover notebooks as this will definitely give more solidity to the confidence-building work you're about to undertake. If you simply use five-in-a-pack cheap pads, you're far more likely to lose them, find someone else has taken them, use a different (but similar-looking one) by mistake, and you'll either lose a lot of your good work, or have it stored all over the place in different notebooks and you may well lose your momentum. The first notebook will be used for completing exercises and making general notes as you work through the book. The second is for your self-esteem toolbox.

Your self-esteem toolbox

Your second notebook is the most important. We hope it will become your bible for life. A good title for this book would be *My Self-Esteem Toolbox*. As you work through *Zero to Hero*, you'll see certain paragraphs or exercises marked as 'Skill for your toolbox'. In your own words, transpose these into your notebook. Tailor them for your personal needs. Then, long after you've put *Zero to Hero* on your bookshelf, you'll have a summary version, specifically for you, of all the tools you need to keep you feeling good about yourself. We hope it will last you a lifetime.

Once you have your tools to hand, take a look at the layout of this book. It's divided into 13 chapters, each dealing with a different aspect of self-confidence. Some will be more relevant to your own life and ideas than others, so you may want to focus on those aspects that seem to reflect your own problems most closely.

Our promise to you

◆ Confidence-building will be interesting.
◆ Some of it will even be fun!
◆ We'll spell things out in a punchy, common-sense way that you'll understand quickly and easily.
◆ You'll see excellent results quickly.
◆ You'll become an expert on the skills to increase confidence, which will hopefully last a lifetime.
◆ We'll stay alongside you every step of the way.
◆ Life will be so much better by the end of all your hard work.

Activity

Put together your self-esteem toolbox

In case you've skimmed through this introduction, please go back to the paragraph headed 'Your self-esteem toolbox' and read it again. Then ensure you put together your self-esteem toolbox. You might decide on a loose-leaf folder for this. Just bear in mind that you want it to be around for a long time, so ensure that it's solid rather than flimsy.

Let's go!

CHAPTER 1

SELF-ESTEEM – WHAT IS IT AND DO YOU HAVE IT?

> ### Today you will learn ...
>
> what self-esteem, or lack of it, is.

What do we mean when we talk about self-esteem? What does it mean to you?

Take a minute to write down a couple of sentences describing what you think it means.

....

....

Most of you (we suspect) will have included some or all of the following in your description:

- An ability to enjoy life to the full
- An ability to cope with life's ups and downs
- Feeling good about yourself
- Feeling that others, in general, like you
- Having a positive attitude
- Having good social skills
- Willingness to give new things a go
- Willingness to take risks
- Able to make difficult decisions
- Able to achieve life goals.

Definition

Look up 'self-esteem' in a dictionary. The Cambridge Dictionary, for example, defines self-esteem as: 'the belief and confidence in your own ability and value', for example 'The compliments she received after the presentation boosted her self-esteem.' In simple terms, self-esteem means having trust and faith in ourselves. Before you can do this, however, you need to like and value yourself. You also need to be able to accept yourself as you are. The Catch 22 situation here is that, if your self-esteem is low, then these are tall orders.

A measurement

Self-esteem is, in essence, a measurement. We rate ourselves against a variety of criteria, and the result is an estimate of our personal view of our value, or worth. The problem is that we tend to rate ourselves very inaccurately and very harshly. This, in turn, leads to low self-esteem, since, based on our negative perceptions, we continue to undervalue ourselves. Worse is to come – once a person believes something to be true, he or she will start to act as if it were. The person will start to gather evidence to support the erroneous belief, while at the same time discounting evidence that fails to support it, so strengthening the negative view of his or her personal value.

This is the self-esteem trap. Many of us fall into it. Would you like to get out of it? Read on...

TOP TIP

- ◆ We need to be aware that measuring our self-esteem through subjectively rating ourselves can lead us to live with low self-esteem based on unhelpful information and reasoning – not truths or facts.

Activity

Remember when you felt confident

Can you remember feeling confident without having excelled at anything special or receiving any positive input, or did you feel that you needed a particular achievement to give you this positive feeling? If not, don't worry – this will have changed by the end of this book.

SELF-ESTEEM – WHAT IS IT AND DO YOU HAVE IT?

Where does our low self-esteem come from? Were we born with it? Did we learn it? Have life events simply conspired against us so that we feel everything we do goes wrong, and we never get that lucky break that would give our confidence a boost?

> **Today you will learn ...**
>
> the possible origins of your own low self-esteem.

Most people do suffer from some element of low self-esteem. Problems develop when our self-esteem plummets so low that it starts preventing us from doing things: 'I'm not trying for the job promotion – I'll never get it anyway', 'I didn't ask so-and-so to go out with me – they'd be sure to say no, and then I'd feel even worse about myself.'

Where does this come from? Finally, a chance to blame the parents!

Blame the parents

♦ Parents often feel criticism encourages the child to be aware of their weaknesses and to try harder.
♦ Parents feel that their own views, built on knowledge and experience, are to be passed down to their offspring. So the child often learns that what they themselves think is 'wrong' while what someone else (the parent) thinks is 'right'.
♦ A father who says, 'You idiot', when his son makes a mistake is unlikely to remember saying it, while the child believes that he's a useless idiot.

We can see how the low self-esteem habit develops – and this is just in the caring, well-adjusted households! Now consider how many children grow up in households where they're regularly vilified, ridiculed and abused.

School

Then there's school to contend with. Woe betide you if you:

◆ Wear glasses
◆ Have red hair
◆ Are slightly overweight or undersized
◆ Wear the wrong brand of trainers
◆ Don't belong to the right gang
◆ Struggle with maths and the teacher admonishes you in front of your classmates
◆ Aren't great at sports and always come last in competitive events.

Can you start to see how hard it is for any of us to grow up feeling particularly good about ourselves?

Activity
Lessons learned in childhood

● Think about the lessons you learned in your childhood. For example, if you're shy with strangers, think about the opportunities you had (or didn't have) to talk to adults in such a way that you felt an 'equal' rather than simply a child. If you find it hard to stand up to people, think about how your parents reacted if you 'rebelled' in any way.

● Look at characteristics you consider personal weaknesses, and see if you can find a time in your childhood where these ideas might have developed.

● Doing this exercise may help you to understand how your low self-esteem gradually developed.

SELF-ESTEEM – WHAT IS IT AND DO YOU HAVE IT?

Notice here that the corrosive power of low self-esteem comes largely from external circumstances. This is natural.

A concept that will help you to overcome this is the idea of self-acceptance. When you adopt the idea of self-acceptance, you start to value yourself in spite of what others think. In the examples we gave you yesterday, low self-esteem has developed, mainly, due to the negative views and comments of important people in our lives. If we can develop enough resilience to value ourselves in spite of what others may think, we'll start to feel much better about ourselves.

This is a journey for most of us to learn as adults, and means that we have to work to make changes in the thoughts about ourselves that we've brought with us from childhood. (In the next chapter of the book you'll learn how to banish these negative thoughts that may have haunted you for a long time.)

A wobbly bike

Self-esteem is a rickety bicycle in that it wobbles a lot. If our mood drops, so can our self-esteem and vice versa. We can also feel especially confident in certain areas of our lives — super-confident even — and yet hopelessly inadequate in others. Some people say to us, 'I'm completely confident in my workplace, but can't seem to sustain any sort of personal relationship and feel a total failure in this area.'

Negative self-rating

Low self-esteem results in feelings of worthlessness, uselessness, and even thoughts that we're 'bad' people. We tend to define these negative senses by using a comparative rating system. For example, we may decide that someone we know is our idea of a 'perfect' person, and we compare ourselves very unfavourably against this paragon. We also tend to give ourselves 'global' ratings ('so-and-so is a much better person than I am') rather than specific ratings ('so-and-so is more attractive than me, but I can play the piano better'), which would be more realistic.

TOP TIP

◆   Developing the idea of liking ourselves 'no matter what' will give us a much stronger base for self-esteem than being dependent on our achievements and external feedback.

Believe in yourself

●   Can you identify any personal characteristics or behaviours where you genuinely believe, 'This is me, and other people can like it or lump it?'

●   Think about these characteristics for a minute.

●   Do you feel more confident when you take this view? If so, these are genuine feelings. If not, you're probably masking low self-esteem with defiance.

SELF-ESTEEM – WHAT IS IT AND DO YOU HAVE IT?

In our daily lives, most of us experience many events that make us feel good about ourselves. We get good jobs, have loving relationships and create reasonably satisfying lives. So why does low self-esteem not go away for some of us?

> **Today you will learn ...**
>
> to differentiate between beliefs and facts – a vital skill in improving self-esteem.

The answer is the beliefs that we've created about ourselves over many years. The mistake we make is that we then confuse beliefs with facts.

We can't stress strongly enough the importance of grasping this point, and keeping it in mind. We can change beliefs, but we can't change facts.

Activity

Where do our negative beliefs come from?

- Take one negative belief about yourself, for example, 'I'm hopeless at sport'. Next, write down in your notebook where this belief came from. What evidence do you have to support it? Write down at least three different pieces of evidence here – one isn't enough.

- Now think about this for a while, and then write down any evidence you may have to challenge this view. This can be as simple as, 'To be honest, I've never even tried football, so it's only an assumption that I would be useless at it.'

- Don't worry if you find this difficult at this stage. You're simply learning to stretch your thinking at this point and to appreciate the difference between beliefs and hard facts.

CASE STUDY

Melissa was a bright student at school. However, her home life was poor, with an absent father and a mother who escaped her own inadequacies by drinking heavily. When drunk, she became abusive, and Melissa took the brunt of this, for the simple reason that she looked very much like her absent father. When she tried to study at home, her mother told her that her father was stupid, and therefore, so was she, so what was the point of studying?

Melissa managed to keep her mother's beliefs at bay until she got low grades in one of her tests. For the first time, she began to wonder if what her mother told her was true. She then feared her next test, as she realised that – in her own perceptions – perhaps she was rather stupid. Because of this anxiety, Melissa struggled with her next test and did poorly. Melissa now took this as proof that her mother was right. There was no point in trying, as it was a waste of time.

Sadly, Melissa consequently failed at school and achieved very little in her adult life. But, in Melissa's mind, this correctly reflected her low value and status in life, so it never occurred to her to do anything about it.

Melissa's story explains how low self-esteem is maintained. Melissa confused a belief with a fact. When Melissa failed her second test, instead of looking for rational reasons why this might have happened that she could have worked on (being over-anxious, misreading a question, not having studying hard enough, for example), she accepted her stupidity as the root cause of her failure, and her failure as evidence of her stupidity.

TOP TIP

◆ No matter how much we believe negative aspects of ourselves, that doesn't necessarily make them true.

Today you will learn ...

about the gremlin responsible for low self-esteem.

Low self-esteem prevents you from accepting yourself as a valuable person. You can achieve a great deal by way of positive accomplishments in your life, and still suffer from low self-esteem. This is because there's a difference between an acceptance of your abilities on an intellectual level, and an acceptance of yourself on a personal level.

Your personal fault finder (PFF)

The architect of our low self-esteem is our personal fault finder, whose job it is to constantly whisper in our ear, reminding us of our faults and weaknesses. Use your imagination to imagine what your PFF looks like. (Although this may sound childish, bear with us – it's a very helpful tool.) What about a pantomime character – tall and thin in an ill-fitting suit and a huge top hat? Or a little gremlin that sits on your shoulder chattering away to you? Or perhaps an animal – or a radio you can't seem to switch off? You might even want to give your PFF a name. Using imagery in this way will help you to view your critical self as something (or someone) external to yourself that you don't need to keep listening to. In turn, it will be much easier for you to fight something you can visualise and whom you can tell to go away as your self-esteem improves.

Once settled in, our PFF is very hard to dislodge. We learn to live with it and trust and believe what it says. One of the main goals of this book is to enable you to remove your PFF and see it for the fraud that it is. With a little work, this is quite achievable, and you'll be amazed at how differently you'll view yourself without your PFF around to demoralise you.

 TOP TIP

◆ Low self-esteem can persist on a personal level, even when we're accomplishing a great deal at an intellectual level as our personal fault finder (our PFF) works tirelessly to remind us of our faults and weaknesses.

Activity

Describe your PFF

● Write down a description of your personal fault finder. Make it as colourful as you can. The more you bring imagery into play here, the easier it will be for you to deal with your inner critic. Make the caricature humorous, which will also be helpful.

● Now replay in your mind that last critical comment that it made. Does imagining your PFF in this way help you to loosen the extent to which you believe the criticism?

SELF-ESTEEM – WHAT IS IT AND DO YOU HAVE IT?

Today you will learn ...

that the advice of your PFF isn't
serving you well.

Your PFF is a dangerous friend. Not only can it constantly remind you of perceived weaknesses, failures and inabilities, it also encourages you to believe that it's protecting you from harm. In turn, your self-esteem becomes even lower – and your PFF has you just where it wants you.

Examples of your PFF at work

◆ Your PFF constantly reminds you that you're useless, worthless and valueless. These feelings are so upsetting and painful, that finding a way to relieve them becomes vital. But how? The answer your PFF has up its sleeve is to set very high goals for yourself. Surely, if you can gain workplace promotion, become the perfect partner, lose weight, look fantastic, become good at a new hobby or interest, then – your PFF tells you – you'll stop feeling this way about yourself? By relying on these impossible goals to make you feel better, you consistently fail and your self-esteem plummets even lower.

◆ Your PFF tells you that others will probably reject you and that it will be very painful. The solution is to predict your rejection in advance, and therefore take steps to avoid it happening. Your PFF helps you to predict this rejection by telling you, 'You won't get the promotion and it will be completely humiliating – best not to even go for it', 'If you say anything at the committee meeting, others will see how little grasp you have of the facts. Perhaps it would be best to resign?', 'You can tell that your lover is losing interest – he was looking at the TV guide while you were speaking to him. It's obviously over, so why not ditch him first?'

◆ Your PFF encourages you to feel that avoiding rejection is better than experiencing it. The downside is, of course, that you fail to see that your negative predictions may have been wrong – you might have got the job, become chair of the committee, married your lover, who knows?

TOP TIP

- ◆ Your PFF not only feeds you negative information, it offers solutions that are tempting to you since they reduce your anxiety and assist you in avoidance of perceived difficult situations. But, while reducing anxiety, your self-esteem is also reduced and your negative perceptions re-enforced.

Activity

When is your PFF at work?

- When is your own personal fault finder most active at the minute? Think of an area of your life where your confidence is low.

- What is your PFF telling you?

- What solutions does it come up with?

- How do these affect you?

- Does your self-esteem increase as a result of taking your PFF's advice?

- If not, why not?

SELF-ESTEEM – WHAT IS IT AND DO YOU HAVE IT?

13

> **Today you will learn ...**
>
> that your PFF's 'solutions' will entrench your low self-esteem.

Fear of failure is a favourite topic of conversation for your PFF. It spends a great deal of time telling you not only that you probably will fail, but that it will also be unacceptable if you do. Its solution is that you're better off not trying in the first place.

Imagine learning to ski, and being told you're good enough to go up into the next class. Your PFF immediately steps in and questions this. Supposing that isn't true? Supposing you can't cope, fall, injure yourself, make an idiot of yourself? You start to feel really anxious about improving your skiing. Perhaps you'd do better not to give it a go, as you may fail ... Yes, that's the answer! Don't even bother. Stay with the beginners' group. How do you feel now? Relaxed – the anxiety is gone. What a relief! But you're still no good at skiing, and now, you never will be. No chance of increased self-esteem in this area – you'll always be telling friends how you found you were 'no good at skiing'.

The importance of risk-taking

The saying, 'To risk nothing is to risk everything' is very powerful. We must learn to assess risk, manage risk and take risks, or we'll never move forward in life. We need to learn that there is no such thing as failure – there are only successes and learning experiences. It simply doesn't matter if we're not the best at everything, or sometimes make mistakes. But the PFF won't let you see things this way, in case you make some positive discoveries about yourself. So it heightens your anxiety and fear of failing to the point that it seems quite unbearable for you to do so. Your PFF achieves this by running you down, then offering 'solutions' that appear to help, but which, in fact, nail your self-esteem coffin right down.

Your personal fault finder (PFF) is a false friend, and in the course of this book you'll learn to silence it, for ever.

SELF-ESTEEM – WHAT IS IT AND DO YOU HAVE IT?

TOP TIP

◆ Challenge any fear of failure that your PFF builds up by reminding yourself that there is no such thing as failure unless you choose to believe so. However, there are successes and there are learning experiences.

Activity
Examine your fear of failure

Can you think of any examples in your own life where your fear of failure has stopped you from achieving things? Looking back, how do you feel about that now?

Now think about two or three times when you were really frightened, but did the task or faced the fear anyway.

● How did you feel afterwards if you gave it a go and failed?

● How did you feel afterwards if you succeeded?

● Which of these occasions was the most positive?

● Which was the least positive? Why?

SELF-ESTEEM – WHAT IS IT AND DO YOU HAVE IT?

One of the saddest aspects of low self-esteem is that it tends to alienate us from others. We may believe that we have so little value that it's not worth making an effort with people, or we tend to take on a 'victim' mantle, where we feel that life has been very unfair to us.

> **Today you will learn ...**
>
> some of the (possibly familiar) negative character traits that accompany low self-esteem.

Today and tomorrow we will look at some common examples of how low self-esteem can affect how we think and behave. Put a tick beside any that you recognise in yourself.

It's everyone else

We tend to blame other people for our misfortunes: 'I wouldn't have done this, if he hadn't said that'. We decide that we have been unfairly treated, without considering why. We absorb 'magic' ideas such as, 'All the bad things always happen to me'. The more inadequate we feel, the more critical we become – it's as though finding fault with others helps us build ourselves up.

Pay attention to me!

Sufferers of low self-esteem rely on feedback from others to make themselves feel good. They feel miffed and upset if this attention isn't forthcoming. An example would be one partner at a party being berated by the other partner for not paying them enough attention while they themselves were spending a lot of time talking to others. This is low self-esteem talking.

Selfishness

Low self-esteem can breed selfishness. We become so self-absorbed, so wrapped up in our own needs and desires that we have little time to consider the needs and interests of others, even those we love and care for.

SELF-ESTEEM – WHAT IS IT AND DO YOU HAVE IT?

Coffee or tea?

We're so unsure of our ability to make a good decision that we dither, procrastinate and become totally indecisive. This can lead to poor decision-making skills, which, in turn, re-enforce our low self-esteem.

Are any bells ringing so far? Tomorrow explores a few more suggestions, and then you'll need to own up!

⊚⫸ TOP TIP

♦ Don't be embarrassed to be honest here. It will help you to have a good awareness of these characteristics since they reduce your self-esteem. Identifying them is a positive step towards stopping doing them.

Activity

Be aware of your character traits

● Start to think about whether any of these character traits apply to you – or, at least, whether you've been there on the odd occasion.

● We'll ask you to think about this more once you've read the next chapter.

SELF-ESTEEM – WHAT IS IT AND DO YOU HAVE IT?

Poor me ☐

This is the victim mentality we referred to at the start of the chapter. It can manifest itself in two ways:

> **Today you will learn ...**
>
> that once you honestly recognise these characteristics, it will be much easier to stop them.

◆ First, we tell ourselves that we're the victims of circumstances that are outside our control, which stops us taking responsibility for what's happening and allows other people to push us around a bit. There is a saying: 'Other people treat us as well as we allow them to treat us'. It makes a lot of sense.
◆ Second, we may even find comfort in being a victim. We feel it will make people feel sorry for us, and so pay us more attention.

Boastfulness ☐

When we feel inadequate compared to those around us, we may try to put this right by overdoing things in the wrong way. For example, we may name drop, refer to recent personal success stories, or speak in an unnatural way. The idea is to impress others and make them think more of us. In reality, we do ourselves a disservice and impress no-one.

Over-competitiveness ☐

Our need to be right all the time stems from a desperate need to prove ourselves to those around us. Logically, it's extraordinary to believe that beating everyone else at everything would give us more acceptance and approval from others. Yet, this is a form that low self-esteem can take for many people.

These are just some (not all) of the ways that, in our attempts to increase our self-esteem, we end up lowering it even further. Please don't feel an outcast if you recognise some of these traits in yourself. We've all been guilty of some of these things at one time or another. That's human nature. It's the extent to which we behave in these ways that can blight our lives.

TOP TIP

♦ We need to learn to accept ourselves as being just fine as we are in order to get rid of these negative traits. It isn't nearly as difficult as you might think.

Activity
Recognise your character traits

● Be really honest. Do any of the traits from today and yesterday apply to you?

● Don't feel defensive about this. We all tend, from time to time, to try to boost our self-esteem using inappropriate tools. But it's very important to recognise what we do, and to acknowledge it, before we can start to correct it.

● How many of these traits ring a bell with you?

SELF-ESTEEM – WHAT IS IT AND DO YOU HAVE IT?

> **Today you will learn ...**
>
> about a concept you may not
> have thought about before!

Can you think of anyone you know who treats everyone else as an equal, and usually says exactly what's on their mind? A person who appears confident but not arrogant? A person who seems to keep any mistakes that they make in perspective, who can listen or talk, work or relax, and seems constantly at ease?

You might say – if you have someone in mind – that this friend has high self-esteem or is very confident. Yet what we're describing here is a much more valuable commodity – that of self-acceptance. This person is one who accepts themselves entirely as they are, and doesn't waste precious time worrying about what they're not. They'll still strive to achieve what they want from life, and to live it to the best of their abilities, but they don't constantly compare themselves with others who do more, or beat themselves up when they try and fail, or when they make mistakes.

Doesn't that sound a good way to be? Would you like to be like that too? You can learn how.

Being smart isn't everything

If we can only feel good about ourselves when someone else praises us, or when we get a job promotion, this leaves us in desperate straits when we get criticised or ignored, or passed over for the job we want.

TOP TIP

- Not feeling bad about yourself is just as vital as feeling good about yourself. This is one aspect of self-acceptance, and is valuable as it's a permanent state – not one that fluctuates according to how the outside world is treating you at any given moment. It's therefore a commodity well worth developing.

Feeling good without feeling bad

Self-acceptance will come to your rescue. You can make the distinction between valuing yourself as a person, no matter what, and accepting that being a fallible human being who messes up from time to time is quite OK. This is the heart of self-acceptance. If we fail at a task, it doesn't mean we're a total failure. If we act stupidly, it doesn't make us a stupid person. Self-acceptance strongly acknowledges the difference between who we are and our behaviour.

We'll be incorporating the ideas of self-acceptance into this book, alongside self-esteem, to give your view of yourself an extra stability, no matter what the external circumstances.

Activity

Self-acceptance and self-esteem

- Using your notebook, write down a couple of features of good self-esteem, as you see them.

- Now that you've read a little bit about self-acceptance, write down a couple of features of this attribute.

- What differences do you notice between the two?

SELF-ESTEEM – WHAT IS IT AND DO YOU HAVE IT?

> **Today you will learn ...**
>
> that you're perhaps a little more confident about yourself than you thought.

Even when you feel your self-esteem is very low, some of these negative feelings come from discounting your strengths and abilities, rather than not having any.

Testing, testing

Answer the questions below by agreeing or disagreeing with the statements. Score 4 for totally agree, 3 for agree most of the time, 2 for agree sometimes, 1 for agree occasionally, and 0 for never agree. At the bottom of the test, add up your scores.

1 I consider myself to be a fairly worthwhile person. ☐

2 I can take criticism reasonably well. ☐

3 I don't take remarks people make too personally. ☐

4 I try to encourage myself rather than criticise myself for my weaknesses. ☐

5 When I make mistakes, I don't see myself as a total failure. ☐

6 I expect most people to like me. ☐

7 I'm socially confident. ☐

8 I make some contribution to society, even if only a small one. ☐

9 It doesn't especially upset me if others disagree with my views. ☐

10 While being aware of my shortcomings, I quite like myself. ☐

11 I feel that my life is fairly well on track. ☐

12 I can usually deal positively with setbacks. ☐

13 I try not to compare myself with other people. ☐

14 I have a sense of humour and can laugh at myself. ☐

15 I generally consider that life is interesting and fun. ☐

Total score ☐

SELF-ESTEEM – WHAT IS IT AND DO YOU HAVE IT?

22

Your score

A perfect 60: You *may* have a problem! Self-esteem that's too high can be as dysfunctional as self-esteem that's too low (see Day 12). But otherwise, wow, well done!

45–59: Why are you reading this book? You don't really need to, although you're bound to find some tips in here useful, as we could all do with a boost sometimes.

30–45: You certainly need a boost, but you recognise some of your good points, so making positive adjustments shouldn't be too difficult for you.

15–30: You're suffering unnecessarily from negative thinking about yourself. We hope that will have changed totally by the time you've worked through this book.

0–15: You have a very serious self-esteem problem. This book may be enough to help you, but if not, you might benefit from professional help.

⊙⤙ TOP TIP

- ◆ You may find that, when you measure you self-esteem, it's not all bad. Don't worry if you had a poor result – you really can make positive changes.

Activity Rethink the test

- ● Look at the test again. Were you perhaps rather hard on yourself? This is a common feature of low self-esteem.

- ● Consider your answers again, thinking of any times when you've perhaps felt a little more positively than you initially thought.

- ● Now, think whether you have any other qualities of a similar nature that you could add to this list?

SELF-ESTEEM – WHAT IS IT AND DO YOU HAVE IT?

DAY 12: WHAT IS A WORTHWHILE PERSON?

The first question we asked you to consider yesterday was whether you believe you're a worthwhile person.

Is your idea of a person who is worthwhile someone who is kind to others, makes a contribu-

> **Today you will learn …**
>
> how worthwhile you already are … and that too much self-esteem is bad for you!

tion to society, is devoted to their family? Perhaps somebody who has a spiritual or religious leaning, who has been successful career-wise, has created financial stability and shares this with others? In other words, quite a paragon of virtue!

Is it any wonder that if we set one of our personal goals as 'being worthwhile', we could be aiming to achieve the equivalent of climbing Mount Everest without oxygen?

You already have value

One of the goals of this book is to encourage you to realise that you're someone of great value just because you exist. While you'll learn to make positive changes, these will be to enhance your self worth, not to create it.

Yesterday, we also mentioned the fact that self-esteem can be too high, and that this is as detrimental as low self-esteem. Why do you think this might be? Jot down your answers.

....

....

⌖ TOP TIP

◆ You're already a very worthwhile person just because you exist. You simply need to learn to believe it. Too much self-esteem is less attractive than simply accepting yourself 'warts and all'.

SELF-ESTEEM – WHAT IS IT AND DO YOU HAVE IT?

24

An overblown sense of self-esteem

We see all around us the results of people whose overblown sense of self-esteem, which we may call self-importance, has caused their downfall. There are numerous disgraced politicians, sports stars and other well known celebrities who have been so convinced of their superiority that they have underestimated the worth, intelligence and moral values held by others in their actions and deeds.

Aim to feel happy with yourself in spite of your weaknesses, and you'll like yourself just as much as someone who scored 60 on yesterday's test. More importantly, though, others will like you a lot more – and you won't end up on the front pages of any newspapers for the wrong reasons!

Activity

Too big for their boots?

- Can you think of any examples of people you know who really think too much of themselves? How do you feel about them? Would you prefer to have their view of life or your own?

- How much do you consider that you might already be worthwhile? Start to focus on what you have in the here and now, not your future goals.

- Write down how you might consider yourself to be worthwhile, based on the definition of it in today's lesson.

SELF-ESTEEM – WHAT IS IT AND DO YOU HAVE IT?

25

Today you will learn ...

that we may be using the hidden benefits of low self-esteem to justify staying as we are.

The case study below provides one of many examples of the perceived benefits of low self-esteem. Provided we play the victim, we find that others will feel sorry for us, will rescue us and smooth our path through life. Being a victim can be quite predatory – we tend to hunt down those whom we feel will give us the best response to our sorry tale and focus on trying to get them to help us out.

CASE STUDY

Peter worked hard to establish his own painting and decorating business. He owns a spacious flat and has a good social life. Then an old friend of his got in touch, telling Peter that he was out of work and looking for somewhere to stay on a temporary basis. Out of past friendship, Peter immediately invited Jim to stay with him while he got back on his feet.

But Jim didn't get back on his feet. Having been turned down for a few job interviews, he got discouraged and felt he was unemployable. Jim told Peter that he had no confidence with girls, so Peter introduced Jim to his friends, and tried to set him up on some dates. Jim told Peter that he would love to go on holiday, but feeling so low about himself he just didn't have the confidence to ask anyone – and then of course, there was the cost as well ... Peter again felt sorry for Jim and offered to go away with him himself, and to foot the bill for them both.

By now, Jim was so settled into staying at the flat, he was treating it like his own. He had no bills to pay, an easy life, he wasn't developing any social skills – he shied away from mixing as he felt others would make him feel inadequate – and above all, he had a friend who worried about him and catered to most of his needs.

SELF-ESTEEM – WHAT IS IT AND DO YOU HAVE IT?

It's important to recognise this possibility and learn to identify it honestly if you find yourself using low self-esteem to gain attention or sympathy.

TOP TIP

♦ There can be a pay-off for staying in the low self-esteem zone, if we can use it to encourage sympathy and attention from others. The downside of this is that we never develop self-reliance and a positive thinking style that helps us to accept ourselves without this sort of external input.

Activity

Check out the pay-offs

● Do you ever use low self-esteem to gain attention from others?

● When was the last time this happened – be honest?

● What was the outcome?

● How do you feel about this now – in the light of what you're learning in this book?

SELF-ESTEEM – WHAT IS IT AND DO YOU HAVE IT?

A phenomenon of life – as many people have experienced – is how long it takes us to build up some sort of reasonable self-confidence or 'OK-ness' about ourselves, and yet, it takes only a few seconds to lose all our gains and feel bad about ourselves again!

> **Today you will learn ...**
>
> why your self-esteem is like a ship on a rough sea.

We can be swinging along the road quite happily, feeling great, excited about the next step and then, guess what? We inadvertently catch sight of our reflection in a shop window. Suddenly, we see that our hair looks a mess, our nose is too long, the general impression is just, well, not great. The spring goes out of our step and we start pondering that we're not attractive enough. Our confidence drains away, and the day doesn't seem so exciting and full of potential any more.

Your PFF – driving your view of yourself

Does the above scenario sound familiar? Why do you think this happens? Your personal fault finder – or PFF – is at work again.

The reason that your PFF is so powerful is that it's hard at work all the time. It rarely takes a break or goes on holiday. Because it works all day every day, you become conditioned to believe this inner critic. Your PFF defines how you see yourself. Therefore, you'll only feel good about yourself if you can silence it, or block it out somehow. This is possible up to a point. You may feel that you can prove it wrong by achieving something positive – losing weight, for example, winning a competition, receiving praise at work, wearing a designer outfit that you know looks good. But these feel-good factors only last for so long.

This is because they're *external*. Your PFF isn't in charge of externals. It's in charge of *your view of yourself*. This is a crucial point to remember.

TOP TIP

◆ Our PFF ensures that we're conditioned to think negatively about ourselves, which is why it's so hard to gain confidence, and so very easy to lose it again. We'll defeat our PFF not by constantly achieving external successes to counteract it, but by becoming so comfortable with ourselves that it becomes useless and disappears.

Activity

When did your PFF last strike?

● Think back over the last two weeks.

● Jot down a time when you felt really good about yourself.

● How long did that last? Write down any negative thoughts about yourself that brought your mood back down again.

● Did you actually feel that it was more 'normal' to feel less confident in yourself?

● If so, you're stuck in a low self-esteem rut, and have been neatly placed there by your PFF.

SELF-ESTEEM – WHAT IS IT AND DO YOU HAVE IT?

Here's a test that half of respondents usually find easy and half find very difficult. Guess who finds it difficult? The test will be your activity for today, so if you want to put it aside until you have at least 15 minutes of free time, do so.

Today you will learn ...

that your view of yourself *may* be inaccurate.

Activity How do you see yourself?

First get out your notebook and a pen. Then take your watch off your wrist and set it beside you. We need you to time yourself as you do this test, so don't start until you have made a note of the start time. For the first part of this test, start now.

In your notebook please list your Top Ten weaknesses or faults.

As soon as you have finished, stop the clock! How long did that take you? Make a note below.

Time taken ....

Take a new sheet of paper, start the clock again, and complete the second part of this test.

List your Top Ten qualities and strengths.

Stop the clock again. Record the time taken.

Time taken ....

What have you discovered?

It's likely that:

a) You found the first part of the test much easier than the second part.
b) You might have preferred more space for the first part of the test, but were scratching about to find ten points for the second part.
c) Your time record will show that you took a lot longer to finish the second part of the test than the first.

What does this tell you?

◆ That you're a person with hundreds of faults and few good qualities?
or
◆ That your view of yourself is defined by a negative-thinking style that you may be aware of, but feel you can't do anything about?

The second view is almost certainly going to be the real problem, but it doesn't matter whether you believe either the first or the second view. All that matters is that you're comfortable with yourself – *however you are*. This is the core concept that you'll learn as you work through this book. Once you start to truly accept yourself, you'll start to like yourself as well.

TOP TIP

◆ Life is as good as your relationship with yourself.

SELF-ESTEEM – WHAT IS IT AND DO YOU HAVE IT?

Today you will learn ...

to start focusing on the positive changes to your life that good self-esteem may achieve.

This introductory chapter should have given you a good idea of where low self-esteem comes from, what keeps you hooked into it, and the consequences – and even benefits – of suffering from it.

◆ You've made the acquaintance of your PFF, and are keen to shake it off.

◆ You've begun to realise that your opinions about yourself may be learned from your childhood and skewed, and that they don't necessarily provide a fair reflection of your self-worth.

◆ Most importantly, you'll hopefully have grasped that self-acceptance will kill low self-esteem stone dead.

Before moving on, it's important that you set some goals.

This may seem a slightly strange suggestion after much of this chapter has promoted the idea of being 'OK as you are' and accepting yourself, rather than relentlessly trying to change things. However, feeling OK and accepting yourself doesn't mean that we give up on achieving goals – it simply means that we're still perfectly acceptable people if we don't achieve them, rather than useless duffers.

To illustrate this, it's hard to beat the lines from Rudyard Kipling's famous poem 'If', quoted below. Good self-esteem isn't about winning all the time. It's about being gracious in defeat. It's about accepting yourself even when you lose – and using the loss as part of the learning curve, rather than retiring in despair.

> 'If you can meet with triumph and disaster, and treat these two impostors just the same...' Rudyard Kipling, author

There's also a difference between improving your skills – for which you need a book to teach you the skills you want to improve, for example, *Beginners' Bridge* or *How to Win at Rugby*, etc. – and improving your self, which means learning to like yourself more. You'll need to make some alterations and adjustments in order to do this, but they'll have little to do with achievements and everything to do with creating a heart and a soul that you enjoy spending time with – and which belongs to you.

Tomorrow you'll define your goals more clearly.

TOP TIP

♦ Thinking less about improving your skills and more about improving your self – which may mean your perceptions of yourself – will help you to set worthwhile self-esteem goals.

Activity
Goal-setting for improving your self-esteem

● Have you had any ideas about how you might improve your self-esteem? What were they? Did they include improving skills and abilities?

● In your notebook, write a sentence or two to describe what you now understand as good goal-setting for self-esteem.

SELF-ESTEEM – WHAT IS IT AND DO YOU HAVE IT?

Today you will learn ...

to focus on exactly what you'd like to achieve, by defining it precisely.

Here's a question, known as 'the miracle question', which makes goal-setting much easier:

If we could promise you that when you wake up tomorrow you wouldn't have low self-esteem any more, but would feel supremely confident about yourself, how would you know that this had happened?

SKILL FOR YOUR TOOLBOX

1

Use your self-esteem toolbox to write down your answer to this question. Come up with at least four things that would be immediately different for you. What changes would you notice in yourself (or in others) that would make it clear that the miracle had happened? The answers should highlight your own personal goals. For example, if you wrote:

'I'd be able to talk to the attractive women at the bus stop', then a personal goal might be:

a) to find it easier to socialise with people I don't know, or
b) to find a stable and meaningful relationship, or
c) to have more self-confidence in all situations.

If you wrote, 'My boss would praise my contribution to the department a lot more', then a personal goal might be:

a) to achieve more in my career, or
b) to have more confidence in the quality of the work I produce, or
c) to think of myself as successful in the workplace.

If you wrote, 'I'd receive more compliments about my looks', then a personal goal might be:

a) to feel better about my body image, or
b) to make more effort to look good, or
c) to dress more attractively.

Activity Write down your goals

Write down four major personal goals that you'd like to achieve with improved self-esteem. You don't need to write down more than four because, once you've achieved these four, you'll have mastered the skills to enable you to achieve all of your goals without difficulty. This is because goal-setting is about giving you a personal focus – something to aim for. In reality, the skills you'll learn will be generic – you can apply them in any situation, so you don't need to specify them all now. It won't matter!

Write your personal goals below:

1 ....

2 ....

3 ....

4 ....

Now let's move on to the next chapter, to start achieving them.

SELF-ESTEEM – WHAT IS IT AND DO YOU HAVE IT?

Refresh your memory

Before moving on, make sure that you're taking some learning points from this chapter with you. Write down the five most important points you've picked up, or now have greater awareness of:

1 ....

2 ....

3 ....

4 ....

5 ....

Instant confidence booster

Decide to do at least one small kindness for someone today – up to three if you can. It can be as small as bringing a colleague a cup of coffee, or taking a sick friend some flowers.
Do it. You'll feel great!

What's in your toolbox?

At the end of each chapter we'll be asking you to check your toolbox and ensure you're practising the skills inside it. This will give your self-esteem a boost very quickly. So far, there's just one inside. But if there's anything you've read that you think might be helpful and would like to put in as well, then do so (using your self-esteem toolbox).

TOOLBOX
Items currently inside
1

CHAPTER 2

THINK YOUR WAY OUT OF LOW SELF-ESTEEM

Low self-esteem can be triggered by a succession of failures, for which we blame ourselves, or a chronic 'drip, drip' of having been told, throughout our childhoods, that we're not up to much.

> **Today you will learn ...**
>
> to identify when your low self-esteem started.

For some, it's been an all-pervading part of their lives for as long as they can remember. For others, good self-esteem was taken for granted, until an event, or series of events, changed all that. Many people say, 'I used to feel fine about myself. Then that all changed ...' They'll usually identify:

◆ A time frame, for example, 'A couple of years ago ...'
◆ An event, for example, 'When a relationship broke up ... '
◆ A period in their lives, for example, 'When I went to university ...'.

Activity

What's your view of your self-esteem?

Take a minute to think about your view of your own low self-esteem. Is it a general feeling about yourself? Have you always felt this way? Or can you point to a specific time or event in your life when you first lost your natural self-confidence?

The answer to this question will help you to identify whether your problem is:

● **Unhelpful thinking** – where you've taken a negative view of events that have happened to you, and incorporated these thoughts into your day-to-day thinking style. For example, you always thought of yourself as attractive until someone you cared for deeply ended a relationship, when you decided you must be unlovable; or, you always considered yourself as intelligent until you failed an exam, when you realised that you weren't so smart.

- **Unhelpful beliefs** – where your opinion of yourself is defined by more absolute views, usually developed in childhood, that you consider to be facts. For example, 'I'm a selfish person', 'I can't get on with others', 'I'll never make a success of my life'.

Don't worry too much which you believe your problem to be – you may even think it's a mixture of the two. You'll still be able to get rid of your personal fault finder just as easily.

Now write down what conclusion you came to. If you used to feel OK about yourself, what changed that? If you've always felt poorly about yourself, what beliefs do you actually have?

TOP TIP

◆ Recalling what triggered your low self-esteem can provide useful insight.

THINK YOUR WAY OUT OF LOW SELF-ESTEEM

To learn how to feel good about yourself, you need to learn a little about the way your mind operates.

When you're feeling down and have doubts, people often tell you to 'think positively' and 'look on the bright side'. Imagine if it were as easy as this! Do you sometimes feel like answering, 'Look, I would if I could'. Or do you sometimes agree and try to do as you've been advised?

Today you will learn ...

that to simply 'think positively' isn't the answer. Your thought processes are more complex than that.

On the basis of this advice, how is it that by saying to ourselves over and over, 'I'm *not* selfish' or, 'I'm *very* attractive', or whatever, our self-esteem is unlikely to rise?

'You can transcend all negativity when you realise that the only power it has over you is your belief in it.' Eileen Caddy, author

 TOP TIP

◆   Self-esteem can be lowered by unhelpful thinking about events, or mistaken beliefs that we've carried with us for years and we're certain that they're true. Either way, we can learn to challenge these problems and to feel perfectly good about ourselves.

Why do you think this doesn't work?

The answer lies in the fact that our thoughts don't hold any water when they're in direct contradiction to our basic beliefs about ourselves. These beliefs aren't *necessarily* true (although they might be) but we *think* they are, which is the problem. You could have film-star good looks, but if you believe, 'I have a big nose that makes my face look ugly', then it really doesn't matter how many times you tell yourself that you're good looking, you're wasting your time. You'll never believe it.

THINK YOUR WAY OUT OF LOW SELF-ESTEEM

SKILL FOR YOUR TOOLBOX

2

So don't do it! You need to start to check out whether your beliefs are true. Do you really have a big nose, or is that what you see when you look in the mirror because someone at school once rudely suggested that you had? Does it really make you look ugly, or is that an assumption you've made – 'If I have a big nose then I must be ugly'?

Sometimes, our beliefs are right – in which case we can problem-solve to make realistic changes. But challenging our beliefs – 'playing detective' to check their validity – is always the first port of call.

TOP TIP

◆ The age-old advice simply to 'think positively' isn't going to work when your self-esteem is low. Learning to take a second look at your thoughts and beliefs to see how valid they really are is going to be far more helpful in shifting your thinking into a more positive mode, and your self-esteem into higher gear.

Activity
Does thinking positively ever work?

Do you ever try to think positively when your mind is flooded with self-defeating negativity? Does it work for you? Consider when it makes a difference and when it doesn't. When you've read the next three chapters, come back to today's activity, and see if you can give yourself a clear explanation for why this rarely works.

THINK YOUR WAY OUT OF LOW SELF-ESTEEM

What's the difference between negative thoughts, negative assumptions and negative beliefs? This is what you'll be considering over the course of the next three activities.

Negative thoughts

These are the 'top layer' of our thinking. They pop in and out of our minds at the drop of a hat: 'Oh, I've messed up there', 'I think I've just said the wrong thing', 'I can tell he doesn't like me', 'I'll never get this right' – in fact, your PFF in full throttle!

Characteristics of negative thoughts

- They spring to mind without any effort.
- They're event-specific, i.e. something happens to cause us to think this way.
- They're easy to believe.
- They can be difficult to stop.
- They're unhelpful.
- They keep your self-esteem low and make it difficult to change.
- They're often not true!

These negative thoughts may be difficult to spot to start with, as you're probably not always aware that you have them (or you may define them as 'rational' thinking and see nothing negative about them), so the first step is to learn to recognise them.

Just becoming aware of these thoughts can help you start to think in a more helpful, constructive way.

But thoughts alone aren't the whole story – there are two further layers of thinking that prevent you feeling good about yourself.

⊚ TOP TIP

◆ We mistake negative thinking for rational thinking. Learning to spot self-defeating thoughts is the first step in getting rid of them.

Consider your negative thoughts

● Write down what you consider to be negative characteristics about yourself. Presumably you consider these to be rational thoughts.

● Now see how many 'ticks' these thoughts get when you measure them against the characteristics of negative thoughts listed opposite.

● What might this mean about your thinking?

THINK YOUR WAY OUT OF LOW SELF-ESTEEM

Negative beliefs

Negative beliefs are the 'bottom layer' of our thinking. We regard them as absolute – they're not open to debate as, in our minds, they're simply facts. We can have negative beliefs about:

Today you will learn ...

how negative beliefs trap us in low self-esteem mode.

◆ Ourselves ('I'm worthless')
◆ Others ('People always let you down')
◆ The world ('Crime is everywhere')
◆ The future ('Nothing will ever change').

Negative beliefs can be so deep that we rarely even consider them. We see them as absolute truths – 'just the way things are' – but they're very often wrong. Usually stemming from childhood, when we rarely – if ever – question what we learn, they keep us trapped in our low self-esteem.

CASE STUDY

Anne's parents loved her very dearly, but decided that it would be beneficial to tell her that whatever she achieved, she could do even better. However well Anne did, instead of being praised, they told her to 'try even harder next time'. If she got 80 per cent in a test, that was a failure and she must get 90 per cent next time. If she got 90 per cent then only 100 per cent was good enough. Not surprisingly, Anne developed a negative belief about herself along the lines of 'No matter how hard I try, I'm just not good enough.'

Anne did get herself a good job. But she could never fulfil her potential, since every time she started on a piece of challenging work, her 'I'm just not good enough' belief kicked in and she'd think, 'I won't be able to do a good job. I'll get it wrong and everyone will see how incompetent I am. I'll let someone else take it on, and stick to simple tasks I can't mess up.'

Telling Anne to think more positively that she will do a good job won't help her at all because it flies in the face of her basic belief that she isn't good enough.

You need to learn to identify unhelpful beliefs that prevent you from thinking more positively about yourself and your abilities, and to learn how to replace them with more realistic beliefs that will stop holding you back.

TOP TIP

◆   We're less aware of our negative beliefs than we are of our negative thinking. This is because we convince ourselves that our beliefs are 'truths'. Constantly remind yourself that negative beliefs are no more than a point of view that may not be true.

Activity

Work out your basic beliefs

●   Consider any negative beliefs you might have about yourself. Write them down. Use the criteria listed above to ensure that they are basic beliefs.

●   Ask yourself, at this moment, how strongly you believe each of them, using a scale of 1 = not much and 10 = absolutely.

●   At the end of the book, you can rate them again and see how much the strength of your negative beliefs has diminished.

THINK YOUR WAY OUT OF LOW SELF-ESTEEM

Negative assumptions link our beliefs to our day-to-day thinking. In this sense, they're the 'middle layer' of our thinking. They also become our rules for living.

> **Today you will learn ...**
>
> how assumptions and rules for living keep our unhelpful beliefs in place.

Rules for living

For example, if you hold a negative belief that you're a boring person, then you may make a negative assumption that, 'If I talk to people socially, they will find me dull and uninteresting.' When you get a party invitation, you may think, 'I won't go. No-one will want to talk to me.' Or you may go, but decide, 'I'll just stand by myself in the corner and hope no-one notices me. That way, I won't have to talk to people.'

In time, you may develop a rule for living that it is better not to socialise, as this will stop your 'I'm boring' belief being put to the test.

Anne, from yesterday's case study, with her 'I'm not good enough' belief, might make a negative assumption that, 'If I stay on the bottom rung of the career ladder, doing simple work I can easily handle, then hopefully, I won't lose my job.'

Anne is developing a rule for living that it's better not to do anything that she finds difficult so that her incompetence will never be discovered.

TOP TIP

◆ Becoming aware of the negative assumptions you make, and the rules for living you use as a result, is a good first step towards making positive changes.

THINK YOUR WAY OUT OF LOW SELF-ESTEEM

Identify your rules

Can you identify any rules for living of your own? Look back at any basic beliefs that you managed to identify. Now ask yourself how you cope with those beliefs on a daily basis. For instance, if you believe you're unlikeable, your rule for living might be to be as nice as pie to everyone at all times to compensate for this. Write down three rules for living that you tend to use to help you overcome some of your self-defeating beliefs.

1 ....

2 ....

3 ....

The good news is that, as your self-esteem and self-acceptance increase, you'll be able to throw these rules in the bin. Remember that these thoughts, assumptions and beliefs are usually wrong, and that it's not too hard to replace them with more helpful, accurate and positive alternatives.

Activity

Examine your self-defeating thoughts

- Write down one or two recent self-defeating thoughts you've had. Now see if you can work out what assumptions you're making for that thought to seem valid, and what basic belief might be lurking in the background. Do you have a rule for living to cope with this?

- If you can, have a go at this exercise a few times so that you can identify these connected mistaken ideas more easily.

THINK YOUR WAY OUT OF LOW SELF-ESTEEM

Thoughts don't upset us

Having negative thoughts isn't what upsets us. It's the *emotions* such thoughts can generate that upset us. If you think you're a 'born loser' but the feeling that this generates for you is calm acceptance (unlikely, but bear with

> **Today you will learn ...**
>
> that low self-esteem isn't generated by adverse events, but by the way we interpret these events.

it for the sake of example), you'll feel OK. If the feeling that this thought generates is total despair, then you'll feel anything but OK.

Low self-esteem is problematic because it makes us *feel* bad about ourselves. Your thoughts generate these feelings. According to U.S. psychologist Dr David Burns, 'You feel the way you think.'

At this point, you may well want to protest. You may still believe that the way you feel about yourself is due to external circumstances – other people failing to give you help and encouragement, poor parenting, lousy circumstances and 'bad breaks' that have caused things to go wrong in your life.

Activity

Consider a different scenario

Jane is waiting in a restaurant for her girlfriend, Liz. They haven't seen each other for several months and Jane was really looking forward to meeting up again. Then she gets a text from Liz to say she's held up at work and will be late. Jane waits on ... but Liz doesn't turn up at all. Jot down how many different interpretations Jane could make of this event.

CASE STUDY

Meet Joel. As he walks down a corridor to his office, he passes Corin. 'Hi Corin,' says Joel, giving him a friendly wave. Corin walks on by and fails to acknowledge Joel at all.

If you were Joel, how would you feel?

- ◆ Upset ('Corin obviously doesn't like me.')
- ◆ Angry ('How rude. He couldn't even be bothered to say hello.')
- ◆ Amused ('Silly idiot – he must have forgotten his glasses.')
- ◆ Concerned ('He was obviously very preoccupied. I wonder if everything's OK?')
- ◆ Easy-going ('Oh well. Corin isn't always over-friendly.')
- ◆ Disappointed ('He didn't notice my new outfit.')

To summarise

One event – two men passing in the corridor.
Six possible different thoughts about the event.
Six possible different feelings ...

SKILL FOR YOUR
TOOLBOX
3

Why didn't the last sentence finish with 'about the event'?

Because the feelings weren't generated by the event. The feelings were generated by the thoughts about the event.

TOP TIP

- ◆ Remember – how we feel is determined less by life events, and more by how we perceive them.

THINK YOUR WAY OUT OF LOW SELF-ESTEEM

Does the idea of separating thoughts from feelings now make more sense to you? This is a crucial point as it's the foundation on which to create good self-esteem. It means that, instead of having to change all your life

Today you will learn ...

to improve your ability to separate thoughts and feelings.

circumstances, you can work on changing your thinking – a much less daunting prospect – and this will change the way you feel.

Activity

Practise 'unpacking' your thoughts and your feelings

- Make a few photocopies of the 'Unpacking your thoughts and feelings' table on page 228.

- Now look back over the last week and write down, using the table, two or three events that have caused you to feel a reasonable level of emotion. See the table opposite as an example. Identify the emotion you felt, and then write down what you were thinking at the time, or just before the event happened. Can you see more clearly how your thinking about the event decided how you felt about it?

- Some people have trouble separating thoughts and feelings. A simple tip is to remember that thoughts usually appear as sentences, for example 'I hope I get this promotion', while feelings are almost always just one word – happy, sad, cheerful, depressed, relaxed, anxious, etc.

- Fill in at least three lines on the table today. Then fill in one a day for the next week.

TOP TIP

- By changing our thinking, we can change the way we feel.

The emotion you felt	The event that triggered this emotion	What you thought when this happened (self-critical thoughts generated by your PFF)
Uselessness	Friend failing to apologise for forgetting appointment	"I'm obviously pretty insignificant in their life."

TOP TIP

- Turn off your personal fault finder and you will feel a lot better.

If someone with low self-esteem gets turned down for a job they really wanted, their PFF may say to them, 'You're useless. You'll never get a good job. There will always be other candidates far better than you.'

Today you will learn ...

how your behaviour affects (and is affected by) your thoughts and feelings.

In this negative-thinking state, what is this person's most likely behavioural response?

The likelihood is that their *behaviour* will mirror their *thinking*.

◆ They may stop applying for jobs at all.
◆ They may set their sights lower, and apply for jobs well below their capabilities.
◆ They may still carry on going for interviews but expect to do badly at them, which will be reflected in the impression they make, or fail to make.

In turn, this means they're likely to stay unemployed – confirming that their negative thoughts and beliefs were correct. This will make them feel emotionally low, and their self-esteem will sink even lower.

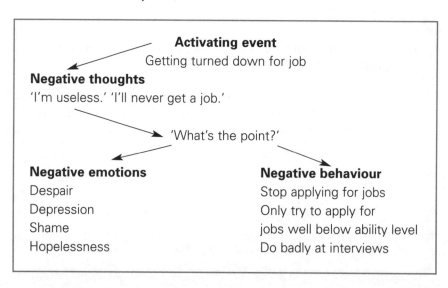

Activating event
Getting turned down for job

Negative thoughts
'I'm useless.' 'I'll never get a job.'

'What's the point?'

Negative emotions
Despair
Depression
Shame
Hopelessness

Negative behaviour
Stop applying for jobs
Only try to apply for
jobs well below ability level
Do badly at interviews

The good news is that we can tap into any one of these areas, make a few small changes, and those changes will have a knock-on effect on the other areas. The diagram below gives you an example.

Thinking
'Getting turned down for this job doesn't
mean that I'll be turned down for all jobs.
There are other jobs out there
– and if I keep trying I will succeed eventually.'

Emotions
Calm
Determined
Relaxed

Behaviour
Keep applying for good jobs
Do research on internet
Investigate study courses

SKILL FOR YOUR
TOOLBOX
4

Whichever of these options you choose to change – and you only need to tinker with one of the three – then the other two will change automatically.

TOP TIP

♦ Negative thoughts and emotions trigger negative behaviours. We're often not aware that these behaviours are self-defeating. Changing any one thing – thinking, feelings, behaviours – will change the others.

Activity
Self-defeating behaviour

Look back at the table from Day 24, listing your negative thoughts and feelings. In the fourth column, now write in a heading, 'Self-defeating behaviour', and write down what you did as a result of your negative thoughts and feelings.

THINK YOUR WAY OUT OF LOW SELF-ESTEEM

'There are no impossible dreams, just our limited perceptions of what's possible.'
Beth Mende Conny, author

Today you will learn ...

a powerful way of combating self-defeating thinking.

You've now learned to identify your self-defeating thoughts, and the emotions and behaviour patterns that go with them. But up to now, your PFF has had the upper hand.

Now's the time to give your PFF a great big kick out of the door!

◎⚹ TOP TIP

♦ Remind yourself strongly that how you feel is based on what you think. If you want to feel good about yourself, you need to think realistically, not negatively.

Use a thought record

SKILL FOR YOUR TOOLBOX
5

The best way to challenge your PFF is by writing down your negative thoughts and emotions, and then writing down more positive or realistic alternatives. This is called a thought record, since although you're recording what's happened, the main focus is on what you *thought* about what happened. The more you practise filling in a thought record, the easier it becomes to spot negative thoughts, and to understand the effect they have on how you feel.

Write it down

Writing things down can be a chore: 'It takes so much time', 'I can never find a pen', 'Can't I just do this in my head?' No – sorry! Writing things down is far more powerful than simply trying to think things through. It causes you to really think hard, and all the time you're writing, you're thinking. Take a look at the example thought record on the opposite page. You'll see that it's an extension of the table you filled in on Day 24. This format will change again (for the last time) on Day 32, so just make one or two copies of this thought record, which you will find on page 229, to use until then.

⊚ TOP TIP

♦ Simply having an awareness of negative thinking (rather than assuming that it's rational thinking) can help us feel better.

Activity

Practise filling in your thought diary

You might want to copy out the following thought record in your notebook, or take a photocopy if you can (see page 229). Then, practise filling it in, working across the page. Fill in each column for at least one negative thought. Don't worry if it doesn't come too easily yet. In the next chapters you'll get further tips and ideas to turn this into a really useful tool.

Date and time, and what happened	What you thought when this happened (How strongly do you believe this? 1–10)	How you felt (How strongly did you feel this? 1–10)	Alternative thoughts (Generate at least 2 or 3 alternatives. Rate your belief in them 1–10)	How do you feel now? (Rate any possible change, now you've looked at things more positively)
Thursday at work. Boss criticised report I had written.	My boss thinks I'm useless. He'd probably like to get rid of me. (10)	Hopeless, despairing (10)	Boss is quite tough and treats others this way as well. (9) My previous work has been excellent. Boss told me so last week. (9)	I still wish I had done better, but I have it in perspective. Feel less hopeless (3) and not despairing at all. (0)

THINK YOUR WAY OUT OF LOW SELF-ESTEEM

Find alternative responses

You may initially find it hard to come up with alternative responses for your thought record. This is because your natural tendency is to be self-critical – and to believe these self-critical thoughts to be true.

Rate your thoughts and emotions

> **Today you will learn ...**
>
> suggestions for getting the most from your thought record.

You'll notice we ask you to rate (subjectively) how strongly you believe your negative thoughts, the intensity of your emotion, and the strength of your belief in the alternative responses.

SKILL FOR YOUR TOOLBOX

6

♦ This is so that you can check that you've picked the thought that gen-erates the emotion.

♦ For example, if your negative thought is, 'I'm over-dressed for this function' and your emotion is 80 per cent panic, you may not have logged the right thought.

♦ Ask yourself *why* being over-dressed is causing you such anxiety and you'll get closer to your real concern. The answer might be, 'I will look completely out of place and everyone will laugh at me.'

♦ Now you've identified the thought that might cause such panic.

♦ This is an important point as your thought record won't help you unless you're working with what really bothers you. So do take some time to consider what's *really* upsetting you.

Be firm!

Be very firm with your rebuttals. Really talk back to your PFF. Come up with at least two or three alternatives, not just one. There are always several different ways of looking at the same thing. Find them.

Lack of belief in the alternative

You may initially find that, although you come up with alternative thoughts, you don't really believe them. You still believe your self-critical thoughts more strongly. This will gradually change — and you'll learn further skills in later activities to help you to re-enforce your beliefs in a more positive outlook.

Rating the strength of your emotions at the end of the thought record checks whether challenging the negative thoughts does in fact help you to feel better.

Once you're familiar with identifying negative thoughts, you can examine how unrealistic or unhelpful they are and whether they're useful to you. Studies have shown that doing this can improve your mood and make you feel more in control of your situation and your life.

TOP TIP

◆ Challenging your self-defeating thoughts is a very powerful way of loosening the grip they have on your self-esteem. Be sure to rebuff these thoughts very strongly.

Activity

Challenge those negative thoughts!

Start using your thought record on a daily basis. Set yourself a goal of challenging one negative thought every day for the next two weeks. As you get more used to doing this, eventually you won't need to write your thoughts down any more, but do make sure you do this initially.

THINK YOUR WAY OUT OF LOW SELF-ESTEEM

> **Today you will learn ...**
>
> to start to identify thinking errors.

The feelings generated by low self-esteem – worthlessness, depression, anxiety, to name but a few – are caused by distorted thinking. Once you learn to challenge these thoughts, you'll immediately change how you feel – both about yourself and life in general.

Negative or rational?

Recognising distorted thinking isn't always easy. We assume that all our thinking is rational and 'correct'. In a good frame of mind this may be true (though not always). But when we're in a poor frame of mind, our thinking can become negative and distorted without our realising that this is happening.

 TOP TIP

> ◆ Feelings generated by low self-esteem – worthlessness, depression, anxiety to name but a few – are caused by *distorted*, rather than rational thinking.

Compounding our thinking errors

The problem is that, once we start making thinking errors, we tend to stick with them. They become – as we've learned already – assumptions and beliefs that we retain unless we make an effort to recognise them and change them.

Psychologists have identified a number of common thinking errors that most of us make some of the time (and some of us make all of the time). If you know what these are, and recognise them, it will make your challenging rebuttals much easier to work out. Over the next few days, place a tick against any you feel apply to you. Here's the first ...

Generalising the specific

You come to a general conclusion based on a single incident or piece of evidence. If you have a minor car accident, you decide you're a dangerous driver (and must never drive again). One failed recipe means you can't cook and wobbly stitching means you can't sew. Someone treats you unfairly and you say, 'Nobody likes me.' You use words such as 'always' and 'never', 'nobody' and 'everyone' to make a general rule out of a specific situation.

SKILL FOR YOUR
TOOLBOX

7

When you challenge your thinking, ask yourself if you're taking a specific situation and making a general assumption about it. Be sure to turn this back to specific thinking. For example, if you make a mistake, don't tell yourself that you're hopeless, tell yourself that you didn't do *that specific thing* as well as usual. If you get rejected, don't tell yourself that you're unlovable, tell yourself that *this particular person* wasn't right for you.

Activity

Look out for distorted thinking patterns

We all use distorted thinking patterns at times. It's very common. With that thought in mind, look at what you've already written in your thought record. Have you made any generalisations about yourself or your behaviour? If so, be sure to come up with an alternative thought that's specific.

THINK YOUR WAY OUT OF LOW SELF-ESTEEM

> **Today you will learn ...**
>
> to identify further thinking errors.

Here are some further common thinking errors to consider.

Mind reading

This is one of the most common thinking errors we make when our self-esteem is low. Without their saying so, we think we know what people are thinking and why they act the way they do. In particular, we can work out how people are feeling towards us. It's fatal to self-esteem because we think that everyone agrees with our negative opinions of ourselves:

◆ 'I know he thinks I'm boring.'
◆ 'I can tell she doesn't like me.'
◆ 'I'm sure they don't really want me in their group.'

Yet we're jumping to conclusions without any real evidence – and, for some reason, we only seem to have the gift of mind reading *negative* views.

SKILL FOR YOUR
TOOLBOX
8

Interestingly, we never seem to develop a talent for mind reading positive thoughts!

Writing such thoughts down in a thought record will help you to re-evaluate this supernatural thinking ability and challenge your mind reading certainties.

Filtering

We take the negative details from a situation and then magnify them, while at the same time filtering out all the positive aspects. For example, you've dressed beautifully for a formal evening and your partner pays you the well-deserved compliment of saying how nice you look. But, as you leave the room he mentions that the hem of your skirt isn't quite straight at the back. You now feel that you don't look lovely any more, and that the evening will be spoiled while you worry about the hem of your dress. The fact that, apart from this, you look stunning passes you by.

Polarised thinking

We think of people, situations or events in extremes such as good or bad – 'I must be perfect or I'm a failure', 'If I'm not beautiful, I'm ugly'. There's no middle ground. The problem is that we usually find ourselves on the negative end of our polarised extremes. So if you can't be perfect, you must be all bad. If you don't get the job you want, your future is ruined. If your relationship doesn't work out, you'll never find true love.

TOP TIP

♦ Identifying distorted thinking patterns is a very helpful way of identifying and challenging self-defeating thinking.

Activity

Recognise your thinking error

● Do you recognise any of the thinking errors above as those that you occasionally (or often) use?

● Look at your thought record again and make a note of any of these that you're using. Are there some that you use more than others, for example, mind reading or filtering?

THINK YOUR WAY OUT OF LOW SELF-ESTEEM

Catastrophising

We expect disaster. We notice or hear about a problem, and immediately hear a catalogue of 'what if's':

◆ 'What if tragedy strikes?'
◆ 'What if it happens to me?'

> **Today you will learn ...**
>
> a few further examples of thinking errors that you may be using regularly and need to identify.

We then decide that if this terrible thing did happen to us, we wouldn't be able to cope.

Personalisation

This involves thinking that everything people do or say is some kind of reaction to us.

◆ Perhaps your partner mentions that your home is looking a little untidy. You'll immediately read this comment as a criticism of your housekeeping skills.
◆ Someone mentions that the work team hasn't achieved its targets this month. You instantly decide that this comment is really directed at you personally.
◆ You find yourself becoming unnecessarily defensive, and possibly even causing ill feeling by taking someone's passing remark as personal criticism.

Blaming

This is the opposite of personalisation. We hold other people, organisations or even the universe responsible for our problems:

◆ 'She's made me feel terrible.'
◆ 'That company ruined my life.'
◆ 'Life is so unfair.'

We feel unable to change our views or our circumstances, as we see ourselves as victims of other people's thoughtlessness and meanness.

It's all my fault

Instead of feeling a victim, you feel responsible for the pain and happiness of everyone around you:

- If your daughter misses a lift taking her to a special occasion, you feel totally to blame for not having chivvied her along (even though she's 17 and has taken the whole afternoon getting ready).
- If your firm loses an important client, you'll find a way to believe that something you did caused this.

SKILL FOR YOUR TOOLBOX 9

Checking out possible thinking errors is another excellent skill to add to your toolbox. Make sure that you use it regularly.

TOP TIP

- While it can be hard to discover that much of your thinking is biased by negative distortions, acknowledging this is the first step to change. The next step is to use this knowledge to help you with your self-esteem.

Activity

Recognise that we all have distorted thinking patterns

Show the activities from Days 28 to 30 to friends, family and/or work colleagues, and in all probability, they'll admit to most of the distorted thinking patterns. How do you feel knowing that most of us make these errors? Is there one particular thinking error you use more than others?

THINK YOUR WAY OUT OF LOW SELF-ESTEEM

Checking for evidence

What goes through you mind when you challenge your PFF and write down more positive, rational alternatives? Many people write diligently, but the

Today you will learn ...

to 'play detective' to check out your thinking.

thought in their mind is, 'I don't really believe this. What I really still believe are the views of my PFF.'

SKILL FOR YOUR TOOLBOX
10

How can you strengthen your belief in your alternative views? There is one extremely helpful tool – thought by many to be the most important 'thought shifter' around – and that's to ask a simple question:

'If this is really true, where's the evidence?'

The case study opposite shows what can happen to us when our self-esteem is low. We focus on the negative and ignore the helpful evidence. Focus on finding this evidence today, and tomorrow we'll look at introducing this element to your thought record.

◎ TOP TIP

- ◆ Always ask yourself, 'What evidence do I have?' Having to provide this will help you to move towards better-balanced thinking, and to believe it more strongly.

Activity

Find the evidence

Practise this skill. Look back to your most recent self-critical thought. Ask yourself what evidence you had to support it. If you were a barrister in a court of law, could you provide evidence against it? What would you say?

CASE STUDY

Jenny was concerned about her job. She'd heard that some redundancies were possible at her firm and she started thinking about her own performance and whether her boss might find a reason to get rid of her. The more she thought about it, the more weaknesses she came up with – being late for an important meeting last week, failing to sign up a new client company that had looked promising – was she losing her grip?

Over lunch with a colleague, Anne, Jenny voiced her concerns. Her friend of course asked Jenny why she was coming to this negative conclusion, and Jenny cited what had happened – her 'evidence' for her pessimistic thinking.

Anne expressed surprise. 'But Jenny, several people were late for that meeting due to the tube strike – it couldn't be helped. And while it was disappointing to lose the client, that may not have been your fault at all – you made an excellent presentation, and there were many possible reasons why the client may not have gone ahead. Now think of all the new business you *have* brought in to the firm this year, which you seem to be discounting.' In essence, Anne was presenting Jenny with evidence to contradict Jenny's self-defeating thoughts. But Jenny hadn't thought of this herself, as she was too focused on her negative views of her abilities.

Today you will learn ...

to collect evidence for both your self-critical thoughts and your more positive thinking.

Where's the evidence?

Look at the full version of your thought record on the opposite page. You'll see that there are now two extra columns.

Evidence for your negative thoughts

The first new column asks you to find evidence to support your PFF's negative comments. For example, if you've looked in the mirror just before going out and thought, 'I look dreadful', where's your evidence? For example:

◆ My hair is a mess. (fix it)
◆ My clothes are all wrong. (change them)
◆ Or do you simply feel low about yourself?

Start with evidence to support your self-critical thoughts. You'll usually find it harder than you think to come up with solid reasoning.

◆ Would, 'Oh, I just do' stand up in a court of law?
◆ What would a judge think of your evidence?
◆ Would the judge accept it or throw it out?

Evidence for alternative thought

SKILL FOR YOUR TOOLBOX

11

The second new column asks you to find evidence for your alternative thinking. Using the example above, an alternative thought might be, 'I really don't look too bad.' It will be easier to believe this if you write in evidence to support it, for example:

◆ 'My partner always tells me I look nice when I get dressed up.'
◆ And/or 'My best friend has asked to borrow this dress next Saturday.'

As you get used to finding evidence for your thinking, it will loosen your PFF's hold on your mind through tangible, logical argument, rather than simply repeating optimistic alternatives that you don't really feel hold water. This is a very powerful skill.

TOP TIP

- *Always* ask, 'Where's the evidence?'

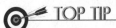

Keep using your thought record

Make several copies of the final (evidence-based) version of the thought record on page 230. Below is an example to help you. It's now a very important tool for you. Use it every time your self-esteem plummets until you start to find that you challenge your thinking without having to write it down.

What happened	What you thought when this happened (How strongly do you believe this? 1–10)	How you felt (How strongly did you feel this? 1–10)	Evidence to support your thoughts	Alternative thoughts (Generate at least 2 or 3 alternatives. Rate your belief in them 1–10)	Evidence to support your thoughts	How do you feel now? (Rate any possible change, now you've looked at things more positively)
Failed driving test	I'll never learn to drive. (generalisation) (8)	Depressed (8)	After 10 lessons, I could not pass.	This does not mean I will never pass. (6) Many people fail their test first time. (6)	My instructor has been very complimentary. My brother failed his test twice and then passed.	A little more optimistic. I will book another test. (9)

THINK YOUR WAY OUT OF LOW SELF-ESTEEM

Today you will learn ...

about a few words you need to put in the bin.

'When we are capable of living in the moment, free from the tyranny of 'shoulds', we will have peaceful hearts.' Joan Borysenko

'Shoulds', 'musts' and 'oughts'

A great deal of negative, self-defeating thinking comes from using the words 'should', 'must' and 'ought'. These words imply personal failure almost every time we use them. They cause us to make demands on ourselves, and suggest that we can't meet those demands:

- ◆ 'I should have known better.'
- ◆ 'I ought to be able to achieve this.'
- ◆ 'I shouldn't have done that.'

This isn't positive thinking

We think this is positive self-talk – that we're motivating ourselves by telling ourselves these things. In fact, the exact opposite happens: 'I should be more such and such (polite, charming, clever, etc.) ... and since I'm not, I then feel badly about myself.'

And it's not only us

When our self-esteem is low, and we feel sorry for ourselves, these 'shoulds', 'musts' and 'oughts' extend to others. People 'should' be nicer to us. Others 'must' consult our opinion when making their plans. Colleagues 'ought' to take into account how busy we are before dumping extra work on our desk.

SKILL FOR YOUR TOOLBOX

12

Now visualise yourself gathering up the words 'should', 'must' and 'ought' and dropping them into the nearest rubbish bin.

THINK YOUR WAY OUT OF LOW SELF-ESTEEM

What can you put in their place?

◆ One option is using acceptance – adopting the idea that it's OK to be fallible ourselves and that others also make mistakes,

◆ You can also replace 'should', 'must' and 'ought' with softer, less absolute and critical language: 'It would be great if I can achieve this, but it's not the end of the world if I don't', 'It would have been better if I'd remembered to … but I'm as fallible as the next person.'

TOP TIP

◆ Put all your inappropriate and stress-inducing 'shoulds', 'musts' and 'oughts' in the rubbish bin – forever!

Activity
Find alternatives to 'should', 'must' and 'ought'

Give this a go. Get out your notebook and write down three sentences using 'should', 'must' or 'ought' in a way that relates to negative thoughts that you had about yourself in a recent situation. Then write the sentences again, having binned the 'shoulds', 'musts' and 'oughts'.

First, your 'should' sentences.

Now, your alternatives.

Did you find that easy or difficult? You now need to practise this a lot. You'll find that your confidence will improve as you stop being quite so hard on yourself (and others).

Focus on how often you use the word 'should', and replace it with a softer option. This should increase your awareness of this thinking error, and encourage you to make the change permanent.

THINK YOUR WAY OUT OF LOW SELF-ESTEEM

Today you will learn ...

how to advise your own best friend.

Almost every one of us has a tendency to be far harder on ourselves than on others. We make allowances for the mistakes of friends and work colleagues. We understand, for others, that a 'bad mistake' doesn't make a 'bad person', but when it comes to ourselves we show no mercy.

SKILL FOR YOUR
TOOLBOX   13

An excellent tool for helping ourselves to be more self-accepting is this. Ask yourself the following questions:

'If my best friend was feeling this way, rather than me, what would I say to them? What evidence would I point out to them to help them see that their pessimistic thoughts or negative self-assessment weren't 100 per cent true?'

The answer you'll probably come up with will usually be quite different to your own, negative self-talk. We're always so much wiser and more constructive at finding positive qualities in others than we are in ourselves. Use your evidence-gathering skills to prove your point, and you will probably find how little evidence there is for the self-defeating thoughts that your 'friend' has.

Another good question to ask yourself is: 'Would my best friend agree with my negative views of myself?' If not, what might they say about you? Most importantly, then ask yourself, 'Why would my friend see me differently to the way I see myself?'

THINK YOUR WAY OUT OF LOW SELF-ESTEEM

Become your own 'best friend'. Use the questions above regularly, and you'll find that it will really help to see yourself and your situation in a more positive way.

⊚⤙ TOP TIP

♦ Always advise yourself exactly as though you're advising your best friend.

 *Activity*

Be your own best friend

● Pick three negative aspects of yourself, or events where you feel that you didn't come up to scratch (as you consider them). Jot them down in your diary.

● Now imagine that your best friend is describing these worries to you. Write down exactly what you'd tell *them*.

● Does this give you a new perspective on your views about yourself?

THINK YOUR WAY OUT OF LOW SELF-ESTEEM

Today you will learn ...

to discover the deeper beliefs that keep your negative thinking going.

You may find it hard to move away from pessimistic thinking if your negative beliefs are deeply entrenched. However, you can still learn to replace these beliefs with a more compassionate and positive view of yourself.

Remember that while our day-to-day self-critical thoughts tend to evolve due to specific events, beliefs we hold about ourselves are absolute. For example, 'I'm boring', 'I'm hopeless', 'I'm unlikeable'.

Can you identify any beliefs you may have about yourself that contribute to your low self-esteem?

If you found that difficult, try the following:

♦ Think back to early experiences that encouraged you to think badly about yourself. What conclusions did you come to about yourself based on events in your childhood?
♦ Think about the things you may do to keep yourself 'safe'. For example, 'I don't socialise much.' Why not? Your answer may help you discover a belief, for example 'I'm boring', 'I can't talk to people.'
♦ Look back at the work you're doing with your thought record. Do you notice any repeating patterns for the critical way(s) you describe yourself? What negative beliefs about yourself do your negative thoughts reflect?

SKILL FOR YOUR
TOOLBOX
14

♦ Use the 'downward arrow' technique. Take any thought from your thought record, and apply the downward arrow technique to it in the following way.

You're worried about a party you've accepted an invitation to, and are starting to feel very nervous.

Your first thought is:
'I'll have a terrible time.'
The first question is:
'Why?'

The answer is:
'I'll feel embarrassed.'
The second question is:
'Why?'
The answer is:
'People will judge me, or won't speak to me.'
The third question is (you're getting it now, aren't you!):
'Why?'
The answer is:
'Because I'm unattractive and boring.'

Using this skill, you've uncovered a belief (two, in fact) that you have about yourself. You can also ask yourself another question: 'What's the personal meaning to me if this does or doesn't happen?' Your answer might be: 'I'm totally unlikeable'.

Once you've identified any basic, self-critical beliefs, you can start chipping away at them, and replacing them with more helpful and realistic, positive beliefs. In this way, your self-esteem and self-acceptance will really increase.

TOP TIP

- ◆ Replacing self-critical (and possibly untrue) beliefs about ourselves with those that are more positive and hopeful will greatly improve self-esteem and self-acceptance.

Activity
Focus on self-critical beliefs

Using your notebook, and using the suggestions made above, continue to look at self-critical beliefs you may have about yourself. Try to focus on beliefs that have been around for a long time. Where they come from childhood, recall any particular critical words that you may have absorbed.

THINK YOUR WAY OUT OF LOW SELF-ESTEEM

'Success seems to be largely a matter of hanging on after others have let go.' William Feather, author

Today you will learn ...

to start focusing on your strengths, rather than your weaknesses.

Start by focusing on your strengths

Now it's time to start focusing on your strengths and your good points.

Revisit Day 15, where we asked you to list ten qualities and strengths. We'd now like you to add a further ten. (You can write them alongside the first ten or jot them all down in your self-esteem toolbox. You'll need to refer back to them so keep them by you.)

It's not impossible

SKILL FOR YOUR TOOLBOX

15

You may find this difficult, but it's not impossible. Write down your smallest achievements, abilities and personal qualities. It's about getting used to focusing on your *strengths* rather than your *weaknesses*. This isn't something you'll normally do, so it won't come naturally or easily – all the more reason for doing it!

For example, look at your working days. Whether you're home-based or office-based, there'll be plenty of examples on a daily basis of things you're quite good at. Perhaps typing, or cooking, keeping things neat, staying calm when others are getting worked up. Once you start thinking over the last week, you shouldn't find it difficult.

Don't rate yourself

Incorporate things you may like about yourself – 'I'm kind', 'I'm patient' – as well as things you can do. Don't rate your abilities and qualities. You don't have to be the best at anything before you write it down. Even having modest abilities at something counts as a positive: 'I don't get too worked up when people are late', 'I managed to stick to my diet for a week' all count.

Refocus

One of the goals of this exercise is to get you to focus differently. Remember what you've learned – it's not who you are or what happened, it's your *perceptions* of who you are or what happened, that define your thinking and your self-esteem. You're now learning to shift your perceptions from negative to positive.

What you've *also* achieved is a collection of evidence to help you ditch your self-critical beliefs. Keep this evidence with you and move on to the next step.

TOP TIP

♦ Focusing on what you like about yourself and what you do well will help you start to see yourself differently.

Activity Compile a list of strengths

Start making your list of strengths – at least 20.

Today you will learn ...

how to replace negative beliefs
with positive ones.

SKILL FOR YOUR
TOOLBOX
16

What's a positive data log?

A positive data log is an excellent tool for getting you to question self-critical beliefs.

It's simple but very effective. Take a negative belief that you hold, and − to start with − find any evidence that you can that might suggest your belief isn't true all the time. You can use some of the evidence that you collected on Day 36. Use and photocopy the table on the opposite page.

An example might be:
Self-critical belief: I'm unlikeable.
Alternative belief: I'm quite likeable.

Evidence to support your alternative belief

... and to show that the self-critical belief isn't true all the time:

- I do have a few friends.
- I've been invited to several social events so far this year.
- In general, people are pleasant to me.
- My work colleagues are friendly.
- I get invited to work social functions.
- I do my best to be kind and thoughtful.
- My neighbour thanked me for my helpfulness.
- I normally have a steady partner, and I've been in two long-term relationships.
- Although I said no, I've had a marriage proposal.
- I'm close to my family.

Small steps

Don't aim for too big a swing from negative belief to positive belief. Changing beliefs can take several months, so a middle-of-the-road alternative will serve you better to start with than an unrealistic, 'I'm totally likeable' belief.

⊚ ✎ **TOP TIP**

◆ Finding evidence to support your more positive belief will give you confidence that it's true.

Activity **Fill in your positive data log**

Start filling in your positive data log. Do two or three, and gradually add to your evidence for each one over a period of a week or two, as you notice events and experiences that support them.

POSITIVE DATA LOG

Self-critical belief: .... New, alternative belief: ....

Evidence to support your new belief and weaken your old belief

1 ....
2 ....
3 ....
4 ....
5 ....
6 ....
7 ....
8 ....
9 ....
10 ....
11 ....
12 ....
13 ....
14 ....
15 ....
16 ....
17 ....
18 ....
19 ....
20 ....

THINK YOUR WAY OUT OF LOW SELF-ESTEEM

> **Today you will learn ...**
>
> how to measure the strength of
> your new beliefs.

Self-critical beliefs take longer to change than our day-to-day, event-specific negative thinking. This is – as you've already learned – because they have been around a lot longer and are more absolute.

Keep your toolbox by you

This is why your toolbox of skills is so important. These are the things you must keep practising, long after you've finished this book. This is what will make all the difference.

But you'll start to see some change fairly quickly, and you'll gain encouragement from using a rating scale to track this.

Rate your improvements

You don't need to see an absolute, i.e. 100 per cent, gain. That would be both difficult to achieve and arrogant! For example, if your original, self-critical belief was, 'I'm unlikeable,' and the belief you'd like to replace it with is, 'I'm likeable most of the time' (note we're not striving for a total opposite, but a realistic alternative), your rating scale might look like this:

Desired belief: 'I'm likeable most of the time.'

Initial strength of that belief (put an X over the percentage):

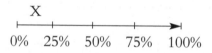

0%   25%   50%   75%   100%

Desired belief: 'I'm likeable most of the time.'

Strength of belief after two weeks of skills practice:

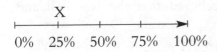

0%   25%   50%   75%   100%

SKILL FOR YOUR
TOOLBOX
17

Of course, these are subjective ratings, but you'll have a very good feel for how you're progressing, and by continuing to use your thought record and positive data log, you'll find that you're gathering more and more evidence to support your new beliefs.

You're training your mind to re-focus on your more positive characteristics, and to re-evaluate the accuracy of your negative beliefs.

TOP TIP

♦ Be patient as you work for change. Don't expect overnight success and then give up because of lack of it. Rating any changes is a very helpful way of seeing some improvement – even if it's only slight, it's a success.

Activity
Rate your desired beliefs

Rate your desired beliefs as you see them now. You may already find that you don't really want to put your X over the zero. Mark on the scale as accurately as you can. What does the fact that not all of your crosses are on zero tell you about your thinking?

THINK YOUR WAY OUT OF LOW SELF-ESTEEM

Today you will learn ...

to check the validity of your beliefs.

You can use simple, practical experiments to test out negative predictions. For example, Mary believed that she was dull and uninteresting. What sort of assumptions or rules for living do you think Mary might have?

Perhaps:

◆ 'If I speak to people, they'll find out how dull and boring I am' (assumption) and

◆ 'I should keep myself to myself so people won't realise how hopeless I am' (rule for living).

SKILL FOR YOUR TOOLBOX

18

Testing out beliefs

Mary was asked to devise some experiments to test out her beliefs, and she came up with the following.

Experiment one

Challenge: make a simple comment to at least ten people – they could include shop assistants, receptionists, the paper girl, etc.

Mary's prediction: 'No-one will speak to me. They'll think I'm odd and I'll feel embarrassed.'

What happened: Six people started a conversation with Mary. Three people smiled at her. One person ignored her comments.

Experiment two

Challenge: Invite a friend to visit the theatre or cinema with you.

Mary's prediction: 'Whoever I ask will make an excuse and I'll feel unlikeable.'

What happened: The first person Mary asked couldn't come, but sounded genuinely disappointed. The second person accepted immediately and thanked Mary for thinking of her.

Experiment three

Challenge: At lunch in the staff canteen, ask to sit with different people every day for a week, and note their responses.

Mary's prediction: 'This will be embarrassing. People will find it hard to say no, and I'll feel like I'm intruding.'

What happened: On one of the days, the person she asked said they were just leaving the table, and on another, the colleagues she chose were engrossed in a work problem and Mary was unable to join in. But, on three of the five days, Mary's colleagues welcomed her and chatted to her with interest. Mary relaxed and enjoyed it. Testing things out encouraged Mary to modify her 'I'm dull and boring' belief to one of 'Some people find me quite interesting'.

Mary could use her experiments to add to her positive data log. If she carries on with her experiments, she may be able to modify this belief even further, perhaps to, 'I seem interesting to most people'.

TOP TIP

♦ Testing out negative predictions is an excellent way to question negative beliefs. The worst that can happen is that it's as bad as you predict, and the likelihood is the outcome is quite different to your negative expectations.

Activity
Devise an experiment

Devise a small experiment for yourself to test out one of your self-critical beliefs. Make it very simple and easy, so that you're not tempted to duck out. Make a prediction, and see what actually happens.

THINK YOUR WAY OUT OF LOW SELF-ESTEEM

Today you will learn ...

a simple skill for helping you to focus on your positive qualities.

Many people suggest that the way to get rid of our PFF is simply to 'think positively'. This isn't entirely without merit. But it's very difficult to do (or we'd all feel remarkably good about ourselves all the time, which isn't the case)!

SKILL FOR YOUR TOOLBOX 19

So how can we structure 'think positively' to give it more of a chance to help us? How do we keep our positive qualities in the forefront of our minds? American psychologist Martin Seligman has come up with an exercise he calls 'the three blessings'. It's adjusted slightly for this book, and renamed as 'bringing your positive qualities into focus'. Professor Seligman has undertaken extensive research in the United States that shows that doing this exercise for as little as one week has a very positive effect on our view of ourselves and life generally.

You may laugh at its simplicity, but consider for a minute why it's so effective.

A simple exercise

At the end of every day, write down three positive things that have happened, that have been caused by a positive quality of your own. The events may be very insignificant, for example, 'The postman smiled at me on my way out.'

The key to this – and the harder thing to do – is to then explain *why* it happened in terms of any positive aspect of yourself.

 TOP TIP

- ◆ Don't dismiss this simple exercise too lightly. It has proven to be very effective.

THINK YOUR WAY OUT OF LOW SELF-ESTEEM

For example, 'The bus driver smiled at me … because I seemed friendly.'

One or two other examples to help you get the idea might be:

◆ 'I brought my work colleague a cup of coffee.' Relating this to a personal quality, you might put, 'I'm a thoughtful person, at least some of the time.'
◆ 'I managed to plumb in the dishwasher. This means that I do have some DIY skills.'

No false modesty

Don't be over-modest in your assessments. If you've done anything reasonably OK, let yourself feel good about it – feeling good about yourself isn't a crime!

Activity

Bringing your positive qualities into focus

Make copies and fill in the 'Highlighting your positive qualities' table on page 231 for at least a week. Use the example below as a guide. Review any changes in your thinking. Ask yourself why this might be making a difference and what you see as the main purpose of this exercise. Ideally, continue with this for the foreseeable future, and be sure to put it in your toolbox.

Date	What happened/what did I do? (three events)	What does this say about me that's positive?
Monday	Bus driver smiled at me.	I must seem a friendly person to him.
	Complimented work colleague on her nice sweater.	I can be thoughtful and kind.
	Got invited to lunch by friend.	Someone wants to spend time with me socially.

THINK YOUR WAY OUT OF LOW SELF-ESTEEM

Refresh your memory

Before moving on, make sure that you're taking something helpful from this chapter with you. Write down the five most important points you've learned, or now have greater awareness of:

1 ....

2 ....

3 ....

4 ....

5 ....

Instant confidence booster

All too often, we focus on what is wrong, instead of what is right about ourselves. Take a minute to sit down and breathe deeply. Now focus only on positive aspects of yourself. Back this up with recent evidence – people who have thanked you for things, or complimented you, or successes you've had. After a few minutes, get on with your day. You'll feel much better.

What's in your toolbox?

You now have 19 skills in your toolbox. Review them and make sure that you're using at least some of them, where you have the chance to do so.

TOOLBOX
Items currently inside
19

CHAPTER

THE PERFECTION TRAP

> **Today you will learn ...**
>
> that there's no such thing as 'perfect'!

Many people's low self-esteem is driven by unhelpful thinking about the standards they should be able to reach in order to feel good about themselves.

Are you one of these people? A common theme is that these people are almost always extremely bright and intelligent, and are usually doing exceedingly well in life. Yet their self-esteem remains low, because they're still not reaching the perfect way of being they believe they should reach.

Perfectionism = setting yourself up for failure

This is because it's almost impossible to get a perfect score. In many cases, it's impossible to know what that would be. For example:

◆ Is there a cast iron, concrete definition for perfect beauty?
◆ Is there one for being a perfect pianist?
◆ Or a perfect mathematician?
◆ What about a perfect parent?
◆ How would you even know if you had reached perfection?
◆ Even being the best in the world at something doesn't mean that you're perfect at it.

So by trying to be perfect, you'll almost certainly fail every time. How is this likely to affect your self-esteem?

Where does perfectionism come from?

Experience shows us that perfectionism usually develops in child-hood, probably from parents who drive a child to constantly do better – 80 per cent should be 90 per cent, 90 per cent should be 100 per cent. Being in the football team wasn't good enough unless you were captain. Playing an instrument required you to practise relentlessly, and then some more. This doesn't mean your parents were unloving, but they felt that by constantly moving the goal posts, you'd try harder and achieve more. The legacy for many young people is they feel that, no matter what they do, it's never good enough.

THE PERFECTION TRAP

Your adult baggage

You carry this with you into adulthood as a self-defeating belief, and – even though you're probably very successful in most areas of your life – you constantly criticise yourself and feel worthless because you aren't doing things perfectly.

You can change

Change isn't too hard – and it's important. Over the next few days you'll learn how to get rid of the menace of being a perfectionist.

TOP TIP

♦   Perfection is impossible to quantify, and therefore all in your mind. Don't see yourself as a failure, but someone who is very able – but just setting the bar too high.

Activity

Do you think you need to be perfect?

If perfectionism is a problem for you, list the areas in which you feel you need to be perfect. Now, if perfection equals 100 per cent, rate how close you are to that for each of the areas you've listed. Now think of two friends or work colleagues, and rate what you consider to be their abilities in these same areas. If their ratings are lower than yours, or the same, are they as anxious about it as you are? Do they mind as much? If not, why not?

THE PERFECTION TRAP

Review your perfectionist beliefs

Today you will learn ...

to check how helpful
perfectionist views really are.

First, write down three beliefs you have about striving for perfection. For example,

♦ 'I must always try to be perfect.'
♦ 'Anything less than complete success is failure.'
♦ 'Others will think less of me if I make mistakes.'
♦ 'I can't live with myself if I let my standards slip.'

Write down three that apply to you:

1 ....
2 ....
3 ....

Now, using the table opposite (which you can photocopy to use again), take each belief in turn and write down what you see as the advantages to you of having this view. On the other side of the table, write down any disadvantages to you of holding this view. For any views where the disadvantages outweigh the advantages, can you come up with an alternative view that might be more helpful? If you can, write it down. If not, don't worry. You'll find this easier by the end of this chapter.

Activity **Perfectionist beliefs**
Do the test opposite. If you wish copy or photocopy the chart so that you can use it again.

THE PERFECTION TRAP

TOP TIP

♦ It's always worth weighing up the pros and cons of your thinking styles, to see if there is a more helpful way to look at things.

Perfectionist view you hold 1	
Advantages of holding this view	Disadvantages of holding this view
Could you find a more helpful view now?	
Perfectionist view you hold 2	
Advantages of holding this view	Disadvantages of holding this view
Could you find a more helpful view now?	
Perfectionist view you hold 3	
Advantages of holding this view	Disadvantages of holding this view
Could you find a more helpful view now?	

THE PERFECTION TRAP

> **Today you will learn ...**
>
> whether non-perfectionism
> equals low self-esteem.

At the end of Day 41 we asked you to consider that friends or colleagues might not share your need to achieve such high standards all the time. What answers did you come up with? Jot them down here:

My friends/colleagues seem happy with achievements that I find inadequate. Why?

1 ....

2 ....

3 ....

4 ....

Now, for each of the reasons you've given, answer another question. Why does this matter? For example, if you've put, 'My colleagues are contented with a lower standard of work', ask yourself why that matters. Use the downward arrow technique that you learned on Day 35.

Activity

Assess your colleagues' approach to perfectionism

Today's activity is similar to yesterday's, but this time focuses on your colleagues' achievements and why they seem contented with less perfection than you. Ask yourself the advantages and disadvantages to *them* of their approach. Then, for each person, make a subjective assessment of their self-esteem (1 = low, 10 = high).

The key question now is: 'What does this tell you?' Write down below what you've discovered and what it might mean.

....

....

DAY 43: THE PERFECTIONIST PERSPECTIVE OF OTHERS

Approach/view of friend/colleague	
Advantage to them of holding this view	Disadvantage to them of holding this view
Subjective self-esteem rating for friend/colleague	
Approach/view of friend/colleague	
Advantage to them of holding this view	Disadvantage to them of holding this view
Subjective self-esteem rating for friend/colleague	
Approach/view of friend/colleague	
Advantage to them of holding this view	Disadvantage to them of holding this view
Subjective self-esteem rating for friend/colleague	

TOP TIP

◆ It's more important to have good self-esteem than to constantly strive for perfection and subsequently burnout. The two ideas don't go hand-in-hand.

DAY 44: CHALLENGE PERFECTIONIST BELIEFS

Today you will learn ...

to look for thinking errors and to consider where your perfectionism came from.

Look again at the beliefs you listed on Day 42. Now go back to Day 28 where we covered distorted-thinking styles. Can you match your views with any of these styles? Remember that these are thinking errors. What thinking errors are you making? We suspect that 'all or nothing thinking' would be one of them. Become aware of the others.

Before you can get rid of perfectionist tendencies, it may be helpful for you to understand how you got them in the first place. While it's possible that your parents were always stretching you to achieve more, there can be other reasons as well. Here is a summary of some of the possibilities:

1 Parents constantly urging you to do better.
2 Desperately needing to please a parent. This might be out of fear, or even love – where, for example, financial sacrifices have been made in order to ensure you received a good education.
3 Sibling rivalry.
4 Scholastic rivalry – perhaps getting into competition with one or two other pupils to 'always be the best'.
5 Feelings of inferiority, either at home or in adult personal relationships that taught you conditional love. (Unless I'm perfect, my family/partner won't care for me.)
6 Being abandoned. This can result in either an, 'I'll show them!' mentality, or throwing yourself into work or academia as a panacea – something that won't harm or distress you.

Write below where you feel your own perfectionist tendencies have come from:

....

....

....

....

THE PERFECTION TRAP

92

Now write a sentence or two describing why you feel that you need to keep this perfectionism going – based on the reason you've worked out above. Do you still need to be perfect? Are the reasons still valid, or are you carrying past beliefs that it would be better to replace?

....

....

....

....

Perspective

One of the biggest thinking errors is to believe that being better than everyone else at everything you do, or beating people at every game there is to be played, is going to make you more likeable.

Hopefully, you'll want to move forward, and tomorrow you'll learn how to replace old perfectionist beliefs with some that are far more helpful to you now.

TOP TIP

◆ Ideas about being perfect come from past experiences that, if we stop and think, often aren't valid anymore. So we don't need to keep following these old rules.

Activity
Work on adjusting your perfectionist beliefs

Selecting the perfectionist thoughts that you've identified in the previous activities, start making a mental note now of how you might positively and helpfully adjust these so as to keep your self-esteem in good shape.

THE PERFECTION TRAP

> **Today you will learn ...**
>
> to shake off perfectionist
> thinking that's based on
> outdated influences.

If you could feel good without always striving for perfection, wouldn't this be much more relaxing?

In the same way that, on Day 42, you weighed up the pros and cons of your perfectionist beliefs. Now you'll do something similar, using what you discovered on Day 44 about the origins of your perfectionism.

Write down what you've decided your own perfectionist beliefs are:

....

What are the advantages of continuing to be driven by this?

....

....

What are the disadvantages of continuing to be driven by this?

....

....

Important point: When answering these questions, bear in mind that you're not being asked to list the advantages of being successful. Rather, we're asking you to think about the advantages of basing your self-esteem on your success.

Is it realistic to carry on thinking in this way? What's the purpose now of continuing to prove something, either to yourself or to others? In other words – don't robotically continue to think, 'I must do things perfectly.' Start to examine what useful purpose this serves.

....

....

Now ask yourself two more things. First, if a friend told you that they felt miserable and inadequate unless they achieved perfection in everything that they did, what would you say to them?

....

....

Second, if you had a friend who seemed to succeed at everything they tried, but came across as rather driven and self-absorbed, would you rate them as someone you really liked?

....

TOP TIP

♦ Striving for perfection won't bring you the satisfaction and likeability that you're looking for. (It hasn't yet, has it?)

Activity

Develop a healthier value system

● Develop a healthier value system by really facing where your perfectionism came from and asking yourself how much you need to keep striving in this way now. Think more in terms of likeability than 'right-ability' as you undertake tasks.

● Check how you feel as you perform tasks, thinking in this new way. Do you feel more relaxed and at ease with yourself? (If you're still having problems, the next chapter will help you.)

THE PERFECTION TRAP

Today you will learn ...

that feeling good isn't always based on perfection.

Perfectionist thinking dictates that satisfaction from doing something is based on how effectively you performed. This isn't true, and testing it out will help you make changes to your life that will be very meaningful.

Activity

Measure your feel-good factor

- Start using a table like the one opposite to subjectively measure your feel-good factor.

- Copy the 'Measuring your feel-good factor' table on page 232 to make a similar table of your own.

- Fill it in at least once a day for the first week, then keep it by you until you really start to make active changes.

SKILL FOR YOUR TOOLBOX

20

Measure your feel-good factor regularly, and you will learn that the greatest pleasure and feelings of satisfaction come from the taking part and not the winning.

TOP TIP

- Let go of the idea that doing things perfectly is the only way to feel good.

THE PERFECTION TRAP

What you have to do	Rate the satisfaction you hope to get from your performance (1–100%)	How much satisfaction did you get? (1–100%) Comment on your rating	Now rate how effectively you think you performed the task (1–100%) Comment on your rating	How do you feel now?
Mend garden fence	20%	90% (can't believe I did it!)	30% (DIY isn't my thing, so it's not the best-done job in the world)	Pretty chuffed!
Give monthly presentation at work	90%	40% (I do this every month, so of course I do it well. I expect it.)	90% (I obviously turn in the best performance I can and am good at my work.)	Pleased it went well, but nothing more.
Game of tennis	60%	90% (I got in a couple of good backhands, and had lots of fun.)	40% (I played poorly, even for my mediocre standard.)	Relaxed and happy. It's only a game, I've had great exercise and a drink with my friends afterwards.

THE PERFECTION TRAP

Refresh your memory

Before moving on, make sure that you're taking something helpful from this chapter with you. Write down below the five most important points you've learned, or now have greater awareness of:

1 ....

2 ....

3 ....

4 ....

5 ....

Instant confidence booster

It's easy to take both ourselves and our lives too seriously. Decide that today you'll find a funny side to everything. Focus on an amusing recent event to get you into a lively mood. Consciously smile as you think about it. Now laugh at yourself when you trip over the cat, instead of swearing; tease the person who's late bringing you something instead of being annoyed; see the irony when the TV recording stops just before the murderer is revealed! Simply find the funny side. You'll feel much better!

What's in your toolbox now?

You now have 20 skills in your toolbox. Review them and make sure that you're using at least some of them, where you have chance to do so.

TOOLBOX
Items currently inside
20

THE PERFECTION TRAP

CHAPTER 4

DEVELOPING
SELF-ACCEPTANCE

Today you will learn ...

how to feel OK in spite of
yourself!

The work you've done so far requires you to look head on at your negative thoughts and to dispute these – to challenge their truth, to look at alternative possibilities, and to seek out evidence to support (in most cases) more balanced thinking.

A different concept and approach

Self-acceptance is a different approach. Instead of arguing with your negative thoughts, you think of them as possibly realistic and truthful – and you may even agree with some them.

'But that is what I'm doing *now*, which is why I feel so badly about myself!'

What's currently happening is that when you acknowledge that you may have faults and weaknesses, you do two things (although you may not notice yourself doing this, as it's simply part of your habitual thinking):

◆ The first is that you generalise the specific – for example, you decide that, since you don't have a scintillating wit, you're a boring person.
◆ The second is you decide that having this weakness is totally unacceptable, resulting in feelings of shame and low self-esteem.

SKILL FOR YOUR
TOOLBOX
21

By contrast, self-acceptance enables you to conquer your personal fault finder by saying, 'That's fine. I don't mind about these particular things I'm no good at. I can accept my shortcomings without diminishing myself.'

If you can learn to do this with calm, inner peace and even a little humour, the results can be quite spectacular.

The secret

The secret is to stop seeing ourselves as a single entity. We're all made up from hundreds of component parts – our skills, abilities, physique, sporting or artistic skills, levels of competitiveness, intelligence, emotional maturity, personal qualities such as kindness, compassion, generosity or meanness, good or poor humour – and many more. If we rated ourselves based on each of these individual strengths and weaknesses, we'd have very varied ratings for them all. Some might be eight or nine out of ten; others perhaps just one or two. If we add up our grand total of individual ratings, the figure we end up with is probably similar to most other people – even though our areas of strengths and weaknesses might be totally different.

TOP TIP

◆ Learn not to generalise the specific. Burning the sausages does not mean you're no good at cooking. It just means that, on this occasion, you burnt the sausages!

Focus on personal skills and characteristics

● Using your toolbox notebook, draw a line down the centre of a page. On one side write down as many personal skills and characteristics as you can think of. In the second column, give yourself a subjective rating out of 10, based on 0 = useless, 10 = my best feature. Don't be falsely modest (you don't have to show this to anyone).

● This activity becomes more interesting if you suggest to another friend or family member that they give it a go as well, using the same basic criteria.

● What do you think you might find out if you do this?

Today you will learn ...

the important distinction between these two types of self-acceptance.

For many people, the idea that they can accept themselves, warts and all, and not stay plunged in low self-esteem seems a paradox. If you already think you're a loser, then surely accepting this is simply throwing in the towel?

Well, that depends. What's described above is unhealthy self-acceptance. Healthy self-acceptance differs from this in several important ways.

Specific weaknesses

Healthy self-acceptance encourages you to accept *specific* weaknesses about yourself – while at the same time rejecting the idea that having these weaknesses makes you an overall no-hoper. People suffering from depression tend to have an unhealthy lack of self-acceptance, and see themselves as generally worthless. A more optimistic personality will reflect only on specific areas of weakness, and not see these weaknesses as meaning that they're not up to scratch as a person.

Don't write yourself off

Someone with an unhealthy lack of self-acceptance will consider their weaknesses shameful, and revert to the idea of global uselessness. Healthy self-acceptance embraces acknowledging your weaknesses but not writing yourself off because of them. You understand that it's OK to have skills deficits, make mistakes, get things wrong, not have the strengths of the next person. But you can say, 'This is called being human, as we all are' and you retain your self-respect.

Personal growth

An unhealthy lack of self-acceptance doesn't encourage change. It allows its followers to stay as they are, lost in self-criticism and low self-esteem. Their ideas conform to the view that there's no point in trying when failure is a certainty. Alternatively they are 'all talk' – the diet/exercise regime/study course starts tomorrow, and tomorrow never comes. Healthy self-acceptance gives you energy and motivation to change. Accepting weaknesses does not mean *retaining* weaknesses. Change is seen as positive, and accepting your shortcomings without any loss of self-esteem will mean that you can meet the challenges it provides you with.

'God grant me the serenity to accept what I cannot change, the courage to change what I can, and the wisdom to know the difference.' Reinhold Niebuhr

TOP TIP

- ◆ It's extremely important to grasp the difference between healthy self-acceptance versus a unhealthy lack of self-acceptance. Make sure you understand it.

Activity

Write down your perceived personal weaknesses

Jot down three or four of your perceived personal weaknesses. Now, for each one, ask yourself two questions:

1 Does having this weakness make me a useless/bad/insignificant person?

2 Am I doing anything towards improving this weakness?

Answering 'yes' to question 1 and 'no' to question 2 means you have an unhealthy lack of self-acceptance. 'No' to 1 and 'yes' to 2 means the opposite – and well done!

DEVELOPING SELF-ACCEPTANCE

Today you will learn ...

an exercise to test your self-acceptance.

Here's a question for you: Is a zebra a black animal with white stripes, or a white animal with black stripes?

Write your answer below:

....

We'll come back to this tomorrow.

Activity Focus on the 'Big I'

- For the purposes of this exercise, the 'Big I' on the right is you! It represents everything about you that makes you a human being. Draw a larger scale version of this 'Big I' on a piece of paper or in your toolbox.

- Now think about qualities that you have – ones that you're aware of yourself, or that your family and friends might consider to be your good points such as intelligence, snappy dresser. Place a small 'i' inside the 'Big I' for each of these.

- Move on to your weaknesses – again, both those that you think you've got and those that family and friends might consider you to have, such as very grumpy when tired, often arrives late. Place further small 'i's inside the 'Big I' for each of these.

- What about neutral aspects of yourself? For example, can cut the grass, dress reasonably, average height, brown hair, don't turn up late too often, etc. Put more small 'i's in for these.

DEVELOPING SELF-ACCEPTANCE

Once you've done all this, your 'Big I' should look like the version on the right.

Of all the weaknesses that came to mind, which one currently bothers you the most? Which one makes you dislike yourself the most, feel ashamed of yourself and wish you were different? Now circle one of the little 'i's to represent this.

Now look again at your 'Big I' – you. The little 'i's within it are the total of you as a human being – good, bad, neutral – warts and all. The circled aspect is just one of many – hundreds, if you took the time to keep working on this.

So does this mean you're a good person or a bad person? A success or a failure? Think about it, and we'll look at this further tomorrow, when we return to the question of the zebra.

The 'Big I, little i' concept was developed by Professor Arnold Lazarus, an award winning psychologist. He often refers to it as 'the egoless self'.

◎⚡ TOP TIP

◆ Keep in mind that you – along with the rest of us – are a complex person with hundreds of different facets and dimensions, strengths and weaknesses. You can choose to tell yourself you're hopeless because of your weaknesses if you want to, but that's far from the truth.

DEVELOPING SELF-ACCEPTANCE

> **Today you will learn ...**
>
> that it's OK to be fallible.

What did you learn from the 'Big I, little i' exercise? Hopefully you'll have gathered that you're far too complex an individual to be able to rate yourself in any one way. This is the principle of self-acceptance – you learn not to rate or evaluate yourself, but to appreciate that you're made up of hundreds of different facets that are constantly changing, and defy any sort of generalised, global assessment of yourself based on these individual facets.

Rate individual aspects

This doesn't mean that you can't rate individual aspects of yourself. Indeed, self-acceptance encourages this, as doing so allows you to consider whether you'd like to make changes and improvements to these aspects – but without running yourself down for having these weaknesses in the first place. For example, perhaps you'd like to improve your time-keeping?

Fallibility

We're all human and so are fallible. We probably make far more mistakes in life than we accept or acknowledge – or even notice. Many of us keep repeating these same mistakes again and again. This doesn't make us bad people, or idiots: it makes us fallible human beings – in other words, normal!

'Humans have an incurable error-making tendency.' Maultsby, psychotherapist and author

DEVELOPING SELF-ACCEPTANCE

The zebra

How did you get on with the question of the zebra? What did you decide? Did it seem impossible to come up with a definite answer? How might that fit in with our current discussion? Could it mean that it's as difficult to say something is either black or white as it is to say that we're personally useless or perfect, nasty or nice, hopeless or wonderful? The answer is 'Yes'!

Before we leave the zebra, you'll remember that on previous days we've referred a great deal to challenging assumptions and finding different ways of thinking about things. The question of the zebra illustrates this beautifully. As you ponder over the issue, consider this:

The zebra is neither a black animal with white stripes, nor a white animal with black stripes – it's a pink animal with black and white stripes.

Never stop looking for an alternative way of thinking about things!

TOP TIP

♦ Fallibility is human. It's fine. It's normal. It simply makes you the same as everyone else.

Fix your weaknesses

● Write down two or three weaknesses that you'd like to fix.

● In the light of what you've learned, how badly do you feel (1 = very bad, 10 = fine) about having these weaknesses?

● Do you think you've been kinder to yourself with these ratings than you might have been before you read these pages on self-acceptance?

DEVELOPING SELF-ACCEPTANCE

> **Today you will learn ...**
>
> a few more simple analogies to explain self-acceptance.

By now, you should be coming round to the idea that you don't have any sort of global rating as a human being, but are simply made up of a huge number of different qualities and characteristics, some of which are strengths, some of which are neutral and some of which are weaknesses. This realisation will hopefully help you to see yourself in a more accepting light.

Here are a few more basic illustrations to ensure you're thinking along the right lines.

The bowl of fruit

Picture a bowl of fruit with all your favourites in it – apples, oranges, pears, grapes, peaches, whichever you like the best. Look at the bowl closely. Wait a minute ... there's a bad fruit in there: a grape with mould or an apple with a wormhole. What will you do? Throw the whole bowl of fruit away or simply throw away the mouldy grape or wormy apple, and keep the rest? If the latter, then why write yourself off as a person, rather than accepting or working on the individual weakness?

The green frog

Stephen Palmer advocates this technique. Imagine that, when you go into work tomorrow, the receptionist tells you that you're a green frog. What a load of nonsense! Then you go to a meeting, and everyone in the meeting tells you that you're a green frog. How absurd! This is obviously a practical joke that your colleagues are all in on. In the evening you go to the theatre, and at the start of the show the compere asks the audience to look around for a green frog. Everyone turns your way. Would you now believe you were a green frog? Probably not, though you might just glance in the mirror. You'd still be more likely to believe that it was a practical joke of some kind.

How interesting it is that when several people tell you that you're a green frog, you're resolute in not believing it. This is because you're retaining your powers of discrimination. Yet when you make a mistake, you label yourself as totally stupid or useless – in other words, you *lose* your powers of discrimination (which would otherwise be telling you that messing up once doesn't mean you're a total idiot).

TOP TIP

♦ Always discriminate between individual weaknesses and your whole being. Don't throw away perfectly good fruit or believe you're a green frog.

Activity
Consider some analogies for self-acceptance

● Think of a few more analogies likes the ones above in order to establish your understanding of the principles.

● Come up with at least three or four to ensure you have got the idea.

DEVELOPING SELF-ACCEPTANCE

Refresh your memory

Before moving on, make sure that you're taking something helpful from this chapter with you. Write down the five most important points you've learned, or now have greater awareness of:

1 ....

2 ....

3 ....

4 ....

5 ....

Instant confidence booster

Visualise it!

What's next on your agenda that's bothering you? When you feel that you may be judged poorly, make a mess of things or simply haven't the confidence to turn up (to a party perhaps?), sit with your eyes closed for a minute and picture the event in your mind, with everything going really well and a successful, happy outcome. Keep doing this until your confidence increases.

What's in your toolbox?

You now have 21 skills in your toolbox. Review them and make sure that you're using at least some of them, where you have a chance to do so.

TOOLBOX
Items currently inside
21

CHAPTER 5

'BUT IT'S NOT MY FAULT – LIFE SEEMS AGAINST ME'

Today you will learn ...

how stuck we feel if we allow
ourselves to become victims.

How you perceive what goes on around you, and how you interpret your abilities to deal with things, has a big impact on self-esteem.

 TOP TIP

◆ Don't blame others for the way you feel about yourself, or look to others for your feel-good factor. Victim mode will leave you helpless to change.

CASE STUDY

Jenny was in a troubled relationship, and her partner, James, had recently moved out of their shared home. Although James had treated her quite cruelly at times, having several affairs and behaving in a moody and erratic way, Jenny's self-esteem was so low that she interpreted this as simply a response to her own hopelessness and unlovability.

Jenny spent a great deal of time telephoning and emailing James, begging him to come home. She felt that, without him, she was totally unlovable, and that she needed him desperately to restore her confidence.

In the end, James reluctantly agreed to Jenny's pleading, and came back home. But the relationship continued to deteriorate as James didn't really want to be there, and continued to see other women.

Jenny's despair came from feeling absolutely stuck. She felt she had tried as hard as she could in the relationship, and that it was James' cruel treatment that made her feel so poorly about herself. If only James would change, she would feel OK about herself again. Without his input, Jenny felt unable to deal with her life.

This case study illustrates victim mode. 'I feel so badly due to some-one else's behaviour, and need them to change in order to feel better.'

Of course, we may feel better about ourselves when people treat us well, *but we can't rely on this.* The minute we say, 'If he hadn't done that, I wouldn't have felt this way', 'I only acted that way because of the way she behaved', 'If she would only treat me with more respect, I'd feel so much better', we're sunk.

You'll suffer from low self-esteem forever if you blame anyone else for making you feel the way that you do. You may be right – so-and-so may be rude, may have run you down terribly, may have landed you in it, made you look a fool, or whatever. But it's not about what other people do, it's about how you respond to what they do that decides whether you feel a helpless victim or not.

Activity
When did you last act like a victim?

- We all do it sometimes! Think about the last time your PFF really laid into you after someone had let you down – perhaps someone cancelled an engagement with you at the last minute. Did you think of yourself as a victim? In other words, did you feel that the actions of the other person were to blame for how you felt?

- Was this a one-off or do you often feel this way?

- What could you do about it?

'BUT IT'S NOT MY FAULT – LIFE SEEMS AGAINST ME'

Today you will learn ...

that comments aren't always criticism, and criticism isn't always personal.

Somebody makes a comment about liking long hair, and you immediately think they're criticising your new short cut. Your boss tells you that the department is lagging behind completing an important project on time and you assume she's commenting on your own poor performance. You suggest to a friend that you get take-away pizzas tonight, and they pull a face and say, 'No, I really don't fancy pizza.' What you hear is, 'What a rotten choice – can't you think up anything better than that?'

When you over-personalise, you mistakenly feel that you're personally to blame for the perceived negative reactions of others. 'If someone disagrees with me, then I must be wrong, and that makes me stupid.' This isn't good for self-esteem.

SKILL FOR YOUR TOOLBOX
22

It helps to identify these thoughts and counteract them. This involves using some of the broader thinking skills we discussed in earlier chapters.

Tips to avoid over-personalising

◆ Respect the opinions of others, as you hope they will respect yours. You're not stupid if you disagree with them, just as they're not if they disagree with you.
◆ Distinguish between opinion and fact. However strongly either you, or the person talking to you, believe something, that doesn't make it true. There are many different opinions on almost every subject. Opinions are exactly that – simply points of view.
◆ Have confidence in your own views. You don't need to be right all the time – simply having a view shows thoughtful intelligence on your part, and you may have valid reasons/past experiences that mean you're more likely to have formed your opinions in a certain way.

◆ Others have their own problems. Your boss may have been under a lot of pressure from her superior to get this work out, and the friend who didn't want pizza may have been pre-occupied with a relationship difficulty.

◆ Other people don't always react in the best possible way. This has nothing to do with you.

TOP TIP

◆ Start being much more aware of over-personalising the comments of others, and use your thinking skills to review the situation.

Activity

When did you take comments too personally?

● Think back over the last week. Can you identify an occasion when you might have mistakenly taken something too personally?

● What went through your mind?

● Using your notebook, jot down some alternative ways of thinking about this, using some of the skills mentioned above.

● How do you feel now?

Every time you run yourself down, you're indulging in self-pity. Not very attractive, is it?

Self-pity is similar to getting locked into victim mode, except on this occasion you're not blaming others as much as you're blaming yourself – and feeling sorry for yourself.

Self-pity thinking

◆ Why do bad things always happen to me?
◆ Why am I such an idiot?
◆ I'll never be any good.
◆ I always draw the short straw.
◆ I can't get anything right.
◆ I got a bad deal on good looks.

The list could go on ...

You're allowing your personal fault finder free rein, and not even arguing. It's easier to say, 'Poor me' and leave it at that. Don't!

We all have 'wallowing' periods. You're allowed these occasionally. But use them wisely, sparingly, and be aware that you're choosing to do so. This will give you breathing space to pull yourself together and look at what you're doing.

Why self-pity is bad for you

Self-pity doesn't get you anywhere ...

Destructive

Self-pity is totally destructive because it robs us of the chance to make changes. It can also lead to depression. What could be more likely to

'BUT IT'S NOT MY FAULT – LIFE SEEMS AGAINST ME'

take you into dark despair than the idea that everything is against you and that there's nothing you can do about it?

Unattractive

Others may feel sorry for us, but they may also think we're being self-absorbed and poor company. They may consider us to be negative pessimists – someone to be avoided.

Wasted energy

The energy that we waste feeling sorry for ourselves could be much better used in problem solving. Self-defeating worry is physically tiring, without serving any useful purpose.

Prevents us from moving on

Self-pity gives us an excuse to indulge our 'stuckness'. We lose ourselves in self-oriented thoughts instead of action-oriented thoughts, and nothing positive happens. We stay where we are.

TOP TIP

♦ Catch self-pitying thoughts as soon as you can. If you need a little wallowing time, that's fine, but limit it and then become constructive. Don't waste energy.

Activity

When did you last feel sorry for yourself?

When did you last feel sorry for yourself? Why? Do you still feel that way – if not, why not? What did you do to stop your self-pitying thoughts? How did you feel once they'd disappeared?

'BUT IT'S NOT MY FAULT – LIFE SEEMS AGAINST ME'

Today you will learn ...

that taking responsibility for how you feel is empowering.

One of the easiest ways of getting rid of feelings of victimisation or self-pity is to take responsibility for ourselves.

It's not difficult. Look in the mirror and say this: 'I now take full responsibility for my happiness.'

Now say this: 'No-one except myself is responsible for my happiness.' There you go! We do appreciate that it's not quite this easy, but it *almost* is.

CASE STUDY

Jim was walking down the corridor at work, when a colleague coming the other way jostled him, resulting in hot coffee being spilt over Jim's new suit. Instead of apologising, the colleague made a weak joke about it and rushed on, calling back to Jim that he was late for a meeting but that Jim should send him the bill for the dry cleaning. Jim was furious. He was left to clean up the mess, dry himself off, and had to walk into a meeting looking a wreck. In response to a jokey comment made by someone in the meeting concerning Jim's appearance, he hit the roof, and the Chair asked him leave the room and calm down. Jim's anger had taken over. He blamed his colleagues for his wretched day and the anger it had produced that seemed to alienate him from several of them.

Was Jim right? As we're sure you realise, the only person responsible for Jim's anger was Jim himself. No one else can make you feel angry (or any other emotion). You choose to feel that way – *and you can decide not to.*

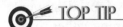

TOP TIP

◆ Don't let other people decide how you're going to behave.

Once we realise that no one else has control over how we feel – and that we have excellent control over how we feel – we can put the lid on negative emotions.

You don't have to put the lid on, of course. If you want to be angry or upset, be angry or upset. But you're choosing to do so, so make these choices through valid thinking, not using 'I couldn't help it' as an excuse.

With the exception of reflex actions such as a knee jerk or blushing, we can control our responses. It may be hard, but it can be done.

Take responsibility. You'll feel much better for it.

TOP TIP

◆ Engrave on your heart, 'I'm responsible for – and decide how – I react. No-one else is.'

Activity
Take responsibility

Do you always take responsibility for your emotions? Look back over the last two weeks (longer, if you need to). Was there a time when you felt very emotional about something? If so, can you remember what thoughts were on your mind? Did they perhaps include the idea that someone or something had made you feel that way? How could you look at that now, taking responsibility for it yourself?

'BUT IT'S NOT MY FAULT – LIFE SEEMS AGAINST ME'

This chapter has looked at our weakness for blaming rather than taking responsibility and making changes, as an explanation for our poor self-esteem. One of the main reasons that people don't change – or not as much as they want to – is that they give up. It's natural to hope that when you open a self-help book, fairy dust will fall out over you to make everything OK, or that reading it once will 'do the trick'. But, like everything else, it's practice that's important.

Giving up can take you back into victim or self-pitying mode:

◆ 'It's too hard.'
◆ 'I don't have time.'
◆ 'It doesn't make sense.'
◆ 'It doesn't work.'

Dr Robert Anthony cites research that shows it takes approximately 21 days to break an old, destructive habit or form a new, positive habit. Please bear this in mind.

It will no doubt take you at least that long to gain positive benefits from what you do. While you're likely to understand the concepts in this book immediately, acting on it is harder. You may read a chapter and say, 'I know that.' But you don't *really* know it.

In order to really know it, it must become part of your thinking, your emotions, your actions and reactions. So unless this is the case, reading something and understanding isn't enough.

To get the best from this book, carry on reading it through in its entirety. Then go back to the entries that deal with specific problems you know you have trouble with. Think about these issues carefully, and most importantly, *act* on the recommendations provided!

This is about taking responsibility for your development. This is how you'll increase your self-esteem. Don't make excuses – that is what victims do – so don't go back into the 'I couldn't help it' syndrome.

You can. You will. And you will succeed.

TOP TIP

◆ Giving up on positive things encourages self-pity. Determine to give your new habits, thinking and behaviours time to develop. Give it 21 days or more – and that means 21 days of working hard!

Activity

What have you given up?

● In the last year, what have you given up and why? Write these things down and think about each one in turn for a minute. There will no doubt be good and valid reasons for some, but not for all.

● When have you used any of the negative thought patterns opposite?

● Do you have any regrets about some of the things you gave up?

● How has this affected your self-esteem?

● What can you learn from this?

'BUT IT'S NOT MY FAULT – LIFE SEEMS AGAINST ME'

Refresh your memory

Before moving on, make sure that you're taking something helpful from this chapter with you. Write down the five most important points you've learned, or now have greater awareness of:

1 ....

2 ....

3 ....

4 ....

5 ....

Instant confidence booster

Pay at least three different people compliments today – more if you can. No excuses if you're at home – ring someone and say something nice during the course of the conversation. How do you feel after you've done this? You should have raised both your feel-good factor (for making someone else feel good) and your self-esteem rating, as you may also get a few compliments back too.

It feels good to be nice sometimes.

What's in your toolbox?

You now have 22 skills in your toolbox. Review them and make sure that you're using at least some of them, where you have the chance to do so.

TOOLBOX
Items currently inside
22

CHAPTER 6

**INCREASE YOUR
CONFIDENCE THROUGH
ASSERTIVENESS**

> **Today you will learn ...**
>
> that it's not what happens, it's
> how you react to what happens
> that causes you to feel good or
> bad about yourself.

Do you feel inadequate when dealing with interpersonal situations that might have any degree of conflict in them? Do you avoid these situations at all costs, feel you're always on the losing end, or show yourself up in a poor light?

Do you currently:

◆ Find yourself getting upset very quickly when others question your opinions and views?
◆ Avoid discussions that might become confrontational, even though it might mean you don't achieve something you need or want?
◆ Say something you then immediately wish you hadn't said?
◆ Agree with the wishes of others – when really you don't agree at all?
◆ Feel your self-esteem constantly dented by your inability to stand up to other people's arguments?

With good self-esteem these thoughts will disappear. Learning assertiveness skills will give you much increased self-confidence. It will also help you to:

◆ Improve your image and credibility
◆ Behave more tactfully
◆ Feel less stressed about confrontation
◆ Achieve desired outcomes in a positive way.

Practise

If you don't already possess these skills – and most people with poor self-esteem don't – then you'll need to practise it a great deal. This in itself may trigger anxiety in some of you, so here's a strategy for making it much easier.

SKILL FOR YOUR
TOOLBOX
23

Get a tape recorder with a good microphone, and you can run through scenarios ahead of the event – again and again if you like – without anyone coming back at you to tell you not to be so foolish.

We often mentally rehearse what we want to say to someone, so how much better to do it so that you can hear how it sounds, and revise it if you need to. Self-criticism in this case isn't another day out for your PFF – it's a constructive move on your part. Listen to how you sound:

- Are you saying too much?
- Or too little?
- Are you sounding too weak?
- Or too strident?

Whatever you don't like, note it, and then start again. Eventually, it will become easy and automatic, and, even if you still feel nervous, that won't stop you from saying what you want to say, and in the right way.

TOP TIP

- Learning to deal with situations in an assertive way, rather than relying on instinct, will develop your self-esteem. You can also practise on your own!

Activity
Practise being assertive

Consider a situation that's coming up that you feel nervous about – possibly a confrontation with your boss, the builders or a family member. Give some thought beforehand to what you need to say, and then use your tape recorder to practise. Do this several times, until you become more confident.

INCREASE YOUR CONFIDENCE THROUGH ASSERTIVENESS

Activity

The assertiveness quiz

Take the test below, which will help you check whether you deal with things assertively or not. Give yourself a score for each statement, ranging from 1 = never, or not like me, 2 = sometimes like me, 3 = always, or very like me. Tot up the scores for each section. Tomorrow we'll examine what your score means.

A

1 When I have to confront someone about a problem I feel very nervous. ☐

2 I'm easily upset or intimidated by ridicule or sarcasm. ☐

3 Being liked by people is very important to me no matter what the cost. ☐

4 I really don't like conflict and will avoid it any way I can. ☐

5 I find it hard to be direct with people if I think they won't like what I have to say. ☐

Total score for this section ☐

B

6 I lose my temper easily. ☐

7 I don't care if people like me as long as I get what I want. ☐

8 I'll use the tone of my voice or sarcasm to get what I want from other people. ☐

9 Patience with people isn't one of my strong points. ☐

INCREASE YOUR CONFIDENCE THROUGH ASSERTIVENESS

10 I often wag my finger at other people to make my point. ☐

Total score for this section ☐

C
11 I can stay calm when faced with sarcasm, ridicule or criticism from others. ☐

12 I'm not frightened of addressing problems directly without casting blame. ☐

13 I'm confident about asking for what I want, or explaining how I feel. ☐

14 I can look other people in the eye when dealing with difficult issues. ☐

15 I feel confident in my ability to handle confrontational work situations. ☐

Total score for this section ☐

D
16 I often make my point by using sarcasm. ☐

17 Rather than speaking out directly to make my feelings known, I'll use impatient or cutting remarks. ☐

18 I show my impatience by my body language. ☐

19 If asked to do something I don't want to, I'll do it, but deliberately won't make any great effort. ☐

20 I use silence to make people realise I'm upset. ☐

Total score for this section ☐

INCREASE YOUR CONFIDENCE THROUGH ASSERTIVENESS

Today you will learn ...

to identify your present behaviour style.

You may have an idea already what your scores tell you. Now let's put them into a specific context so that you have a clearer idea of where you 'fit'.

CASE STUDY

Marian is 42 years old, married with two teenage children, and works part-time in a local office. Her self-esteem is low, and she feels she's neither a good wife, mother or work colleague. At work, she feels over-loaded, and unable to keep up with her volume of work. Because she has little confidence in her work skills, she says nothing, because she's worried that her inadequacies will be exposed if she says she can't manage. The problem is that her colleagues have no idea that she's struggling – they keeping passing more work her way, because she 'never says no'. As a result, Marian doesn't enjoy her job at all, and is constantly worried that she may lose it.

At home, her teenagers are fairly noisy and self-centred, usually untidy, emptying the fridge as soon as Marian fills it and spending more time with their friends than on their school work. Again, Marian fears her inadequacies as a mother are to blame for this behaviour. But in this case, she tries to remedy the situation by shouting at the children, finding fault with their lazy, noisy ways and punishing them with 'no TV' and curfews when they refuse to toe the line. As a result, her relationship with her children is poor. This convinces Marian even more strongly that she's a bad parent.

When Marian's husband comes back from work, Marian feels annoyed that he can't see how stressed she is, and doesn't appreciate the difficulties she has with the children. Instead of saying anything, Marian remains quiet and a little sulky – 'John should be able to tell how I'm feeling' is her view. Unfortunately, John isn't aware, and finds Marian's lack of communication rather hostile. So they spend the evening sitting in different rooms, with no warmth or affection between them at all.

The four behaviour types

The quiz you took on Day 58 aims to work out which of four different behaviour types your actions are closest to. Look back at the quiz. In which section (A, B, C or D) did you obtain the highest numerical score? This will give you an indication as to which of the four categories below you most regularly fall into.

A Passive
B Aggressive
C Assertive
D Passive aggressive

⊙⊰ TOP TIP

◆ You need to identify your present behaviour type before you can adjust to a more assertive style.

 Activity

What are your behaviour styles?

● Using your scores from the test, identify which of the behaviour styles most apply to you. You might find that you're a combination of two or three, rather than always acting in the same way.

● Now look at Marian's story, and identify the behaviour styles she was using in the various areas of her life – none of which did anything for her poor self-esteem.

INCREASE YOUR CONFIDENCE THROUGH ASSERTIVENESS

Today you will learn ...

to identify the detailed characteristics of the four different behaviour styles.

'To compose our character is our duty.' Michel de Montaigne, author

The following four behaviour styles can strengthen or weaken self-esteem.

Passive behaviour

When we behave passively, we tend to 'let things go'. We may totally disagree with what's going on, but we don't say anything as we make a negative prediction that things will

Note: Being passive isn't being easy-going. It's being a doormat.

go against us if we do. If we do speak we're usually disproportionately deferential, full of premature apology, and back down too easily.

Aggressive behaviour

Bullying tactics, rudeness, raised voice, shouting, threats – these are all geared to ensure that the aggressor gets their way on a 'no matter what' basis. You may occasionally have behaved this way yourself, even if you're usually passive. For the passive person, never saying what they mean or asking for what they need can eventually lead to emotional overload. Something snaps and suddenly Sally Shy hits the roof and becomes Bridget Bully.

Assertive behaviour

When you behave assertively, you do two things:

♦ You stay (relatively) calm.
♦ You stand your ground.

You're also happy to hear other people's points of view, as you don't feel threatened or intimidated by them. Valid counter arguments might make you change your point of view, but if not, you clearly stick with what you believe in. You treat others with respect (even if they don't treat you that way). You may be willing to compromise, you speak clearly and you're willing to persist with the discussion until you've all reached a satisfactory outcome.

Passive-aggressive behaviour

One of the most common examples of this is 'the silent treatment'. You'll know just what that is! You may have used it, been on the receiving end of it, or both. This isn't about being overtly aggressive (so it's hard to pin anything on us) but using silence, sulking, leaving a room when the other person walks in, being deliberately obstructive. Passive aggression can also include the 'poor me' treatment – 'I can see I'll obviously have to write that report myself', 'I'm the only one who does anything around here'. The objective of passive aggression is to get your own way by making the other person or people feel guilty.

TOP TIP

♦ Understanding these four different behaviour styles will make it easier for you to behave assertively, which will then increase your self-esteem as you get the results you want in an amicable way.

Activity
How did you behave?

Write down at least one example, from the last week or two, when you think you've behaved in each of the above behaviour styles. Most of us vary, rarely using one style the whole time. Remember how you felt after each event, and rate when you felt the best about yourself afterwards. What can you learn from this?

INCREASE YOUR CONFIDENCE THROUGH ASSERTIVENESS

Today you will learn ...

some skills for thinking assertively.

When dealing with tricky situations, we can make the mistake of gearing our behaviour to our dominant emotions at the time – rather than to the outcome we want to achieve.

When we behave assertively we focus on outcomes and results rather than emotions.

Before you can behave assertively, you need to *think* assertively. This is because you need to be able to consider the outcomes and results you want, ahead of time. These outcomes and results don't simply include getting what you want. They should also include:

◆ How you feel about yourself
◆ How you feel about the other person
◆ How they feel about you
◆ Whether the outcome you've worked for has improved your relationship for the future, enhanced mutual respect, etc. In other words, whether it has left your self-esteem in good shape.

SKILL FOR YOUR
TOOLBOX
24

Thinking assertively is important because it starts off the train of situation-emotions-behaviour-outcome (see opposite), and is a point at which you can maintain control and get the situation to work in your favour, rather than against you.

 TOP TIP

◆ Thinking assertively is as important as behaving assertively. It allows you to focus on outcomes and results, rather than simply running with your emotions and 'seeing what happens'.

Challenge those thoughts

The work on thought-challenging from earlier activities is exactly what you need here.

DAY 61: KEY ASSERTIVENESS SKILLS

Situation

Imagine that you are debating with your partner over holiday destinations for next year. Your partner is insisting on a venue you're not interested in.

Your thinking

Rather than simply feeling upset at the unfairness of your partner's lack of consideration for your views, say to yourself something along the lines of, 'My partner isn't failing to consider me. They're just so keen to go to this place that they're hoping I might get enthusiastic as well. I'll try and understand what they like so much about it, then express my own reservations, and offer some compromises that fit the bill for both of us as closely as possible.'

Your emotions

Instead of feeling distressed, you feel OK.

Your behaviour

Assertive. Listening. You can acknowledge your partner's enthusiastic preference, while focusing on finding a solution to suit you both.

Outcome

Agreement reached, which might be a compromise venue, or the decision that each of you chooses on alternate years, etc. Good relationship maintained. Self-esteem intact!

Activity Negotiate for your outcome

Think of a situation where you'll need to use good negotiating skills to achieve the outcome you want. Now jot down what the outcome is and, using the outline above, write a sentence or two under each heading to show how the negotiation might go, and what thinking skills you'd use to ensure a good outcome.

INCREASE YOUR CONFIDENCE THROUGH ASSERTIVENESS

Once you've mastered these skills, you'll be able to:

◆ Confront difficult issues with others

◆ Stay in control of your emotions while you do this

◆ Stand your ground when the going gets tough.

1 Acknowledge the other person's point of view

SKILL FOR YOUR TOOLBOX 25

Most people will expect you to 'come at them' with your own arguments and views, so they'll be surprised when you start by reflecting on and understanding their problem.

An example might be an unrealistic work deadline your boss has set. An acknowledgement might be, 'The work we're doing now is for our biggest client, and I appreciate your concern that we get this project in on time for them.'

Acknowledging sets the scene for dialogue, rather than confrontation. You're indicating that you're on the same side as your boss, and share his/her goals.

2 State your own position

Now you have to say where you fit in all this. If you really can't meet the deadline, then you could stand your ground on this point. It's often useful to start this step with the word 'however', so you have: 'I appreciate your concern that we get this project in on time for them. However, even if I were to work solely on this project and nothing else, the time-scale would be unachievable if we're to produce good work.'

3 Offer a solution

Sometimes an obvious alternative isn't readily available. But remember that this is about results, and there has to be a solution – even if it's that the work doesn't get done on time. So your thinking needs to move from 'I can't possibly achieve this' to 'What can we do?' and state the possibilities.

Using these steps achieves the following vital things:

◆ It enables mutual understanding of the problems.
◆ It gains the respect of the other person.
◆ It prevents you from being forced to accept an unrealistic/unacceptable/unwanted situation.
◆ It encourages a solution that will suit both parties.
◆ Your emotions don't get the better of you and cause you to feel upset/angry/disappointed, so denting your self-esteem.
◆ The feel-good factor at the outcome is huge, and excellent for confidence-building.

TOP TIP

◆ Think of behaving assertively as a three-step process and do your best to follow this outline.

Activity **Practise being assertive**

Now find a situation and practise being assertive. Use the three steps above every time. You don't need to wait for a major confrontation – even negotiating over a cup of coffee is a good start, and will get you used to it. You may also want to practise this with your tape recorder. Think of possible responses you might get, and work on how to deal with them assertively.

Today you will learn ...

to use assertive skills on yourself, not just with other people.

Learning to be assertive with yourself is as important as learning to be assertive with others.

One of the greatest self-esteem boosters around is the realisation that most of the things you do and think are pretty well the same as what others do and think.

CASE STUDY

Christine saved quite a lot of written work on a CD. The next day, she decided to re-save, using a different filename. Yesterday's disk wasn't labelled (too lazy!), so she used a different one and now she has *two* unlabelled disks. She slips yesterday's disk back into the box (to get rid of it), at the same time thinking, 'You lazy toad. You're making a real mess of your files. Most people would be prepared to put the time in to clean up their CDs and be much more organised.'

How it works...

Using yesterday's model, being assertive with yourself might go as follows:

Acknowledgement

'I appreciate that by putting a used CD back in the box I'm creating a possible muddle for the future.'

My point of view

'But I really can't be bothered about that right now, and it's hardly a terrible mistake.'

Solution

'If I need that CD again in the future, I can just wipe the text off then. I've got so many disks, I may not use it anyway.'

Net result

Responsibility taken for action. Feeling very relaxed and comfortable having reminded self that many, many people do this sort of thing – 'I'm quite OK!'

This is assertive thinking when it applies to you. You have the right to behave however you wish, as long as you take responsibility for it. Most of us sometimes find our fridges full of food beyond its sell-by date (and some of us still eat it!), have messy drawers we never sort out, tell white lies when turning down boring invitations, fail to tidy up the kitchen for days on end until we no longer have a single clean plate, don't ring our mothers enough, keep the fiver we found on the pavement, etc., etc.

That's fine. We're normal. *We're behaving just like everybody else!*

TOP TIP

◆ Constantly recognise and remember not to beat yourself up for what's really very normal, 'everybody does it' behaviour.

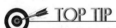

You're not on your own!

● Write down three issues that you allow to consistently lower your self-esteem. For example, 'I get very nervous speaking in a group', 'My house is always untidy', 'I'm overweight'. Any three examples will do.

● Now ask at least three friends, family members or work colleagues (more if you can, for a bigger sample), whether they ever suffer from these problems.

● What can you conclude from your survey?

INCREASE YOUR CONFIDENCE THROUGH ASSERTIVENESS

'We are not the only ones to find ourselves at an apparent impasse. As thousands before us have mastered the worst of troubles, so can we.' Dr R. Brach, philosopher

Today you will learn ...

that you have the right to be both imperfect and OK at the same time.

Thinking assertively means reminding yourself of your basic rights, and then being comfortable with them. You have the right to be a normal, fallible human being, and to ensure you appreciate that this makes you *just like everybody else* and perfectly OK.

Your rights

You have the right:

- To make mistakes – like every other human being
- To be imperfect – again, like every other human being
- To be in charge of your own thoughts, behaviours and emotions (if these are weird and strange from time to time, you're just like everyone else)
- To tell others what you want and how you feel
- To feel OK about yourself even when you're not on top of things
- To use emotional responses sometimes, even when they're not achieving the right outcome (we all do that more often than we might like to admit)
- To put yourself first sometimes (yes, take the last piece of cake, don't help out if you're too tired, read a book while your partner is cleaning the car)
- To stand up for your rights – or not. It's your choice.

Also remember three points:

1 Rights carry responsibilities. If you chose the right to go to bed late, don't grumble when it's hard to get up in the morning.

2 Others have rights as well. Don't let this deter you from saying your piece, but be prepared for the other person to say theirs as well (and that's fine, by the way).

3 See the situation from the other person's point of view as well as your own.

Activity

Get comfortable with your rights

Use the table below to fill in three more examples of rights you consider important to your self-esteem. Use your thought-challenging skills to counter your concerns with some assertive views.

Think of a right	How you view that right with low self-esteem	How to view it with a more assertive viewpoint
I have the right to say how I feel.	What I have to say is probably less important than what others have to say. I will be interrupted, spoken over, ignored.	My views are just as valuable as anyone else's. I will use my assertive skills to overcome interruptions and persist with my point of view, while acknowledging what others have to say.

⌖ TOP TIP

◆ Understanding your rights will help you to be more assertive.

INCREASE YOUR CONFIDENCE THROUGH ASSERTIVENESS

Refresh your memory

Before moving on, make sure that you're taking something helpful from this chapter with you. Write down the five most important points you've learned, or now have greater awareness of:

1 ....

2 ....

3 ....

4 ....

5 ....

Instant confidence booster

When our confidence is low, we can start to worry and become self-critical. This makes us very tense. Breathing deeply, as well as using easy muscle relaxation exercises, will help. Here's a favourite relation skill to use:

● Tense your body up tightly, and try to push your shoulders upwards to touch your ears.

● Keep tensing everything as you count slowly to ten.

● Then relax very quickly, and count slowly to twenty.

● You'll instantly feel much calmer and more confident.

What's in your toolbox now?

TOOLBOX
Items currently inside
25

You now have 25 skills in your toolbox. Review them and make sure that you're using at least some of them, where you have the chance to do so.

CHAPTER 7

ACT YOUR WAY TO
GOOD SELF-ESTEEM

> **Today you will learn ...**
>
> that 'pretending' works!

A good way to improve your self-esteem is to *pretend* to have it. You have to fake it to make it!

Your personal fault finder (PFF) will encourage you to look around at everyone else and it will point out how confident they are, and how hopeless you are by comparison. Today is not about checking the validity of those thoughts – you've hopefully already done a lot of work on that – but rather, to help you learn how to *appear* just as confident as everyone else – many of whom will be 'faking it' successfully, just as you'll be.

A plus of pretending is that, after a while, we don't have to pretend any more. It becomes natural. Telling yourself you're confident when you're not isn't true. But the more you tell it – and in this case, *practise* it – the more you'll believe it. You'll gradually find it easier and easier, and feel less and less self-conscious.

So let's start pretending ...

'We acquire the strength we have overcome.' R.W. Emerson, writer

Confident body language

When we communicate, over 50 per cent of the message we give comes from our body language – non-verbal communication. You can therefore send out confident, positive messages without having to say a word.

How would you recognise confidence from body language? How would you recognise lack of confidence from body language? Jot down a few ideas of your own:

....

....

....

 TOP TIP

> ◆ Use body language to create a confident impression – it will make you feel better, even before you've said a word.

Non-confident body language	Confident body language
Crossing your arms	Open and expansive
Hugging your body	Good posture
Crossing your legs	Leaning towards someone
Placing a hand under your chin	Standing asymmetrically
Stooped posture	Relaxed stance
Standing far from the other person	Leaning towards the other person

Top body language tips

◆ Imagine a string running through your body, right up out of the top of your head. Imagine someone pulling this string tight. This will cause you to stand straighter and taller, which always gives a confident impression.

◆ Clasp your hands casually in front of you – don't fold them across your body. You'll look more relaxed this way.

◆ Give a confident first impression by shaking hands firmly with the other person.

◆ Using hand gestures in moderation can help to convey meaning when you're speaking.

Activity

Practise confident body language

● Practise confident body language in front of the mirror at home. Get an idea of how you look using different stances. You can also use the 'no-no's' to see how unconfident you look in these positions.

● If you want to enlist the help of family or friends, you could ask someone to video you acting out a situation with someone else. This would be particularly useful if there's a special function coming up that's unnerving you.

ACT YOUR WAY TO GOOD SELF-ESTEEM

DAY 66: CULTIVATE A CONFIDENT EXPRESSION

Today you will learn ...

how to show confidence in your face.

Conveying confidence and warmth through your facial expression will make connecting with others much easier.

Eye contact

Eye contact is an important ingredient of this, but can be hard to get right (especially if you feel nervous but are pretending not to be). It's important because it shows that you want to communicate with the other person and are interested in what they have to say. So look people in the eye not only when *you're* speaking, but also when *they* are – this will also help you to gauge their reactions and respond accordingly. Too much eye contact can seem rather aggressive and overpowering; too little can make you seem nervous or embarrassed. A good rule of thumb is to hold eye contact for about 60–70 per cent of the time.

Smile

Smile! Not only does smiling (appropriately, of course) make you appear warm and friendly, research has shown that smiling will help you to feel more self-confident. Picture someone coming towards you with a warm smile on their face. Nothing could convey, 'I'm delighted to see you' more strongly. It's easy to do, and makes a huge difference.

 TOP TIP

- Nothing lights up your face and makes you look more confident than a smile. Make a real effort with this, and you'll see instant rewards.

ACT YOUR WAY TO GOOD SELF-ESTEEM

Relax

Adopt a relaxed and friendly expression. This, of course, can be easier said than done, and has to be linked, up to a point, to your basic personality. If yours is normally not overly expressive, then simply relaxing your facial muscles will work well and will give your face more expression. To help you, a useful trick is to drop your tongue down in your mouth, so that it touches the base of the inside of your front teeth. Now let the muscles of your mouth curve into a very slight smile. Not only will you look relaxed, hopefully, you'll also feel it!

TOP TIP

- Looking and feeling relaxed puts other people at their ease.

Practise facial expressions in the mirror

- Practise facial expressions in the mirror. Say a few words and sentences out loud and be aware of how you look when you say them.

- Have a go at saying things with a smile (where the content would be appropriate) and see what difference that makes to how you look and how you feel as you say the words. You'll find it makes you feel much more confident.

ACT YOUR WAY TO GOOD SELF-ESTEEM

Today you will learn ...

that how you speak is more important than how you look.

This isn't about what you say, but the way that you say it. Nervousness is very audible through the tone of your voice – you may stutter, the pitch may go up or you may speak in a garbled way. When we're anxious – about anything – our breathing becomes shallow as our heart rate rises. This, in turn, affects our speaking voice.

Practise controlling your voice and relaxing to reduce anxiety and nervousness.

Wait your turn

SKILL FOR YOUR TOOLBOX

26

It's better to say nothing than to say too much that sounds bad. Later on in the book (Day 86) you will learn more about active listening; being able to present well without having to say too much. For the moment:

◆ Take a few deep breaths to slow your breathing down.
◆ However nervous you feel, tell yourself that this will pass.
◆ Allow yourself time to relax before you say too much.

Not too loud!

Something else that happens to our voice when we're nervous is that it gets too loud or too soft. Simply becoming aware of this when you're speaking will help you adjust your volume button. You can also ask close family or friends for feedback. Notice what they say, and make the necessary changes. A good tip is to exaggerate your mouth and jaw movements very slightly. This will give your vocal chords the opportunity to move more freely.

Or too fast

Another weakness of nervousness is that we tend to speak too quickly. This is less common than speaking too loudly or too softly, but you need to check whether you do this. You can try and notice this yourself or ask someone else. In our experience, people can't assess for themselves whether they are speaking too fast. Tape recording your voice won't help with this, as you'll be working hard to speak correctly. The answer is to ask a variety of other people who you know will be honest with you.

Keep the pitch low

A low, clear voice indicates confidence, while a high voice will indicate nervousness. Practise varying the pitch of your voice while speaking into a tape recorder. Listen to authoritative speakers such as newsreaders, and notice when they intentionally lower their voices.

⊚ ⟜ TOP TIP

♦ Work hard on your voice until you feel that it has a confident sound to it – even if you're nervous inside, you'll appear relaxed.

Develop awareness of how you speak

Developing awareness of how you speak means lots of practise. Do this in the following ways:

● Think about your tone of voice when you're talking to people.

● Spend some time with your tape recorder – most people are extremely surprised by how they sound. It's not usually what they expected.

● Get family and friends on board if you can – both to comment on your speech in different circumstances, and to role play conversations with you in situations where you find it really difficult to come across well.

ACT YOUR WAY TO GOOD SELF-ESTEEM

Today you will learn ...

how to get those significant 'first impressions' right.

Whatever happens later, first impressions are the most important thing that other people will notice about you – and you them. Think what happens when you meet someone new. You immediately look for signs and signals that will categorise them in your mind. To project confidence yourself, work on the following.

Dress appropriately

SKILL FOR YOUR TOOLBOX 27

Don't think that it doesn't matter how you dress.

It may matter to other people, and only a person who is extremely naturally confident (which we assume you're not) may not care what others think. You *do* want to make a good first impression, because it *will* make you feel more confident. So dress appropriately to the situation. If you really don't know what that is, don't guess – ask somebody.

Do give yourself enough time to ensure you look as good as you want to. Nothing is more discouraging to good self-esteem than ending up in such a rush that you don't have time to change, comb your hair, apply make up. Watch out here for self-sabotage. 'I just didn't have time' is an excuse often used to explain poor appearance, when the thought process is really more to do with, 'What's the point? I'll still look dreadful' or similar negative thinking. In this case, work on your thinking rather than your excuses.

Act confidently

Make sure that your body language shows the same confidence as your facial expression. During the 'first impressions' stage, you'll be judged much more on non-verbal behaviour than on what you say – for example, saying, 'How nice to be here', while your body language is defensive and your face taut with nerves isn't going to wash. People will judge your behaviour more than your comments at this stage.

Other points to focus on to get the first impression right are:

- ◆ A firm handshake – where appropriate (it isn't always, of course) this indicates excellent self-confidence
- ◆ A broad smile – nothing says 'pleased to meet you' better than this
- ◆ Good eye contact.

TOP TIP

- ◆ Focusing on and practising making a good first impression will give you a great deal of initial confidence.

Activity

Replay situations where you felt nervous

Think about social/work situations that make you especially nervous. Now consider the last time you were in one of these situations. Did you make any conscious, pro-active attempt at making a good first impression, or did you simply worry about what impression you might be making? Now replay this situation. What could you have done – or could you do in the future – to make sure that you make a good first impression, whatever you're feeling inside?

ACT YOUR WAY TO GOOD SELF-ESTEEM

Refresh your memory

Before moving on, make sure that you're taking something helpful from this chapter with you. Write down the five most important points you've learned, or now have greater awareness of:

1 ....

2 ....

3 ....

4 ....

5 ....

Instant confidence booster

No matter what your plans are today, first, make the best of your appearance (clothes, hair, etc.). Next, imagine a string coming up through your body, out through your head, and pulled tight – in other words, walk tall!

Finally, make smiling your priority today.

You'll feel terrific!

What's in your toolbox?

You now have 27 skills in your toolbox. Review them and make sure that you're using at least some of them, where you have the chance to do so.

TOOLBOX
Items currently inside
27

CHAPTER 8

BODY IMAGE

Today you will learn ...

that your body image has little to do with what you actually look like.

Having difficulty liking your looks makes it harder to accept yourself, but you don't need to live this way. You can change your relationship with your body from one of active dislike to one of being relaxed and confident with your looks.

Quick quiz

To check whether body image is a problem for you, answer the following questions. For each question, rate your belief in the statement from 0 = not at all to 10 = a lot.

1 Are you uncomfortable with your body in general?

2 Are there aspects of your physical appearance that you really dislike?

3 Do you spend a lot of time worrying about what you look like?

4 Do you think that what you look like plays a big part in whether others like you or not?

5 Do you think that what you look like plays a big part in how much you like yourself?

6 When you think of your looks, do the same negative thoughts keep cropping up?

7 Do these negative thoughts prevent you from enjoying day-to-day life?

8 Do you avoid certain activities or situations (visiting the gym, for example, or going swimming with others) because you feel self-conscious about how you look?

9 Are you considering (or have you had) cosmetic surgery for any part of your body?

10 Do you depend on clothes and/or cosmetics to try and disguise what you consider weaknesses in your appearance?

11 Are you endlessly searching for a new diet, the latest body-shaping exercise, a more flattering hairstyle or dress style?

12 Do you spend a lot of time, effort and money trying to bolster up your 'imperfect' looks?

Your score

0–30: Your body image is good. You don't need to focus on this chapter of the book.

30–60: Your body image is moderately good, and you're not too obsessive about it.

60–90: Your body image is poor and you spend far too much time and effort worrying about it and trying to change your physical appearance.

90–120: Your poor body image could be ruining your life. You could think about getting professional help, if making changes alone seems too hard.

TOP TIP

◆ Your body image has nothing to do with how you look, and everything to do with low self-esteem. This is good news, as low self-esteem is often easier to change than how you look.

Activity What bothers you?

● Write down aspects of your physical appearance that really bother you.

● Do you feel that if you looked better, it would change how you feel about yourself in general?

● Jot down any ideas you have as to how you might deal with this problem.

BODY IMAGE

DAY 70: HOW POOR BODY IMAGE AFFECTS YOU

> **Today you will learn ...**
>
> how poor body image affects you, and where it may come from.

In what ways do you feel that the way you view your physical appearance affects your life? For example, do you consider it responsible for your not having a partner or for your relationship being unhappy? Write down the ways that you think your perceived physical imperfections affect you:

1 ....

2 ....

3 ....

4 ....

5 ....

You may have come up with some of the following:

◆ My self-esteem is lowered generally.
◆ It causes me to feel anxious socially, as I feel that others are negatively judging my looks all the time.
◆ It spoils my sex life, as I hate my partner seeing my body and feel inhibited when making love.
◆ I feel depressed about my looks most of the time.
◆ It has caused me to suffer from eating disorders.
◆ I never feel really feminine/masculine, so feel less attractive to the opposite sex.

Where have these thoughts come from?

A brief answer is that they could have come from lots of different places:

◆ Perhaps you were brought up by image-critical parents.
◆ Perhaps you had unusually good-looking siblings who received more praise than you about their looks.

BODY IMAGE

- Perhaps you've had a bad experience in an intimate relationship, where a partner you loved and admired criticised your looks.
- Perhaps peer pressure in adolescence/early adulthood to look a certain way or follow trends in fashion magazines made you feel unattractive if you didn't meet those standards.
- Perhaps you developed friendships with people who you thought were better looking than you and who received more attention.
- Perhaps you have a distorted way of looking at things, which allows you to make interpretations, such as, 'People would like me more if I was better looking' or, 'My looks are holding me back in life', etc.

Time for improvement

If you've discovered that you have an extremely poor body image, don't worry. This information will help you to make changes. Yesterday's activity asked you to consider any ways that you might deal with the problem. Let's now translate these into an active goal plan for improving your body image and self-esteem.

TOP TIP

- Identifying the particular problems that poor body image gives you is the first step to change. The causes are less important than learning to make changes.

Activity Think it through

It may help you to give at least a little thought to where your poor body image came from, before moving on. Using the suggestions made above, think about your own body image. How did you come to feel the way you do? Was it as a result of one event or a number of them? Do you think that you're alone in this, or that lots of people with poor body image have had the same difficulties?

BODY IMAGE

Today you will learn ...

not to accept negative thoughts about your body image, but to challenge both their validity and importance.

Poor body image is based on negative beliefs and assumptions (remember them from the early part of the book?) rather than reality.

An example of a negative belief (a fairly absolute view) in relation to body image could be, 'Good-looking people are more successful in life.' A negative assumption (more of an 'If ... then' statement) might be 'If I were better looking, then my life would be much happier.' You can challenge these ideas by finding different ways of viewing them or, if your more balanced viewpoint still isn't enough to sway your negative beliefs, you can focus on evidence that simply doesn't support your negative views.

Our goal is to get you to re-think in a positive way both the assumptions you make about your body image and the importance you attach to them. Once you achieve this, your self-esteem will be in good shape again.

Let's take the first example above: 'Good-looking people are more successful in life.' Get out your toolbox and challenge this assumption. How many alternative views can you find? How much evidence can you come up with to disprove this? Write your answers down and then check with our own suggestions (opposite).

Do good looks really matter?

- Good looks are very subjective.
- If good looks are the answer to every good thing in life, why do so many good-looking celebrities suffer from depression, broken relationships, etc.?

- Good looks are a temporary asset. People who have relied on them when young, can find getting older quite difficult.
- We get used to people's looks over a period of time. We can end up not noticing whether they're good looking or not.
- As many tears are found running down the pretty faces as down the plain ones.
- To many people, looks don't matter at all and that isn't the basis on which they judge others.
- Being good looking often prevents people from bothering to develop other qualities needed for a happy life.
- Name some of the most successful people in history. Were/are they good looking?

How many challenges to this statement did you come up with? Now replace the belief we have questioned with a more realistic alternative.

TOP TIP

- As well as challenging possibly erroneous assumptions about your looks, question how valid and important they are, even when they're true.

Activity
Challenge your assumptions

Make sure that you've worked hard on challenging this belief. Add any of our ideas to your list if you missed them. You need to keep these in your self-esteem toolbox, and make sure that you re-read them regularly, until they come to mind more easily.

BODY IMAGE

DAY 72: DITCH NEGATIVE ASSUMPTIONS

> **Today you will learn ...**
>
> to test your body-image assumptions and replace them with more realistic views.

What did you write in yesterday's activity to challenge the statement about looks? Hopefully, it was along the lines of: 'Good looks are nice to have, but they don't account for personal happiness' or, 'If good looks were all-important, only good-looking people would be happy and successful, but that isn't the case at all.' Perhaps you wrote something quite different, but meaningful to you.

Now create a table like the one below (or photocopy this one). You'll use this to record your negative beliefs, find evidence that challenges them, and then, most importantly, replace them with more helpful beliefs about your own looks and the place of looks in society in general.

Challenging beliefs about my body image
My negative belief about my body image or the importance of good looks in society:
Evidence that challenges this belief: 1 .... 2 .... 3 .... 4 .... 5 .... 6 ....
Alternative belief that gives me a more positive view of my body image or the importance of physical appearance in society:
How do I feel about my body image when I look at the subject this way?

BODY IMAGE

To help you, here are some generic examples of the types of beliefs people with poor body image hold. Some may apply to you, and there may be others that you have that aren't listed here. Use the table to cover all of them:

- People judge my character by my looks.
- My life would be much happier if I was better looking.
- I will never be happy until I find a way to change my looks.
- I'm physically unattractive and I know other people see me that way as well.
- My (part of body) is too big, too small, etc. and this is to blame for my low self-esteem.
- There's nothing physically attractive about me at all.

You'll have many negative views specific to yourself. Work through them all.

A wider perspective

If you're agonising over an aspect of your looks, ask yourself this question: What would a starving, homeless person in a developing country say to you, if you told them that these worries dominated your thinking and prevented you from leading a happy life?

TOP TIP

- The more you challenge your negative views relating to your looks, the easier it will be for you to start to like yourself more.

Activity

Focus on challenging your negative beliefs

Fill in at least three different negative belief tables and make sure that you photocopy around a dozen, to use over the next week or so.

BODY IMAGE

Today you will learn ...

that avoiding the negative and focusing on the positive has a powerful effect.

The fairy tale *The Beauty and the Beast* is a great story when you're young. As you get older, you understand the moral behind the story. If you focus less on how you look, and more on developing other positive qualities – or appreciating those you already have – others will see beauty in you.

The error of focusing on the negative

In reality, those of us who worry about our looks are rarely true 'beasts' without a saving grace. The problem is, we focus on our perceived weaknesses and worry about them so much that we fail to see any of our positive attributes. One way of correcting this distorted focus and encouraging you to look at yourself in a more positive light is to re-focus on your good points.

Activity
Find three attractive features

- Every day, for a week, write down in your self-esteem toolbox three physical features that you like about yourself. Now that's a lot of features! Focus on the smallest features – for example, do you like the shape of your ears, the size of your wrists, your ankles? Are your toes well formed? What about your knees? The shape of your nose? You can even turn perceived negatives into positives. If you're female and worry about a small bust, think how nice it is to wear strapless tops without a bra.

SKILL FOR YOUR TOOLBOX
28

- Once you've done this, repeat this exercise on a weekly basis. So, once a week, write down three attractive features about your physical appearance. It doesn't matter if you start repeating features – it's the principle of your thinking that will be changing.

Simple is effective

Don't make the mistake of thinking that this is too simplistic to be meaningful. It can be a very powerful exercise, with long-lasting results. Relish the fact that something so simple can be so effective!

TOP TIP

- Focusing on the positive isn't always something we do naturally, and we need to retrain our minds to work this way more automatically.

BODY IMAGE

Today you will learn ...

how to assess whether to make some positive changes to your looks as well as your thinking.

One of the reasons why you may have a poor body image is the reality that what you see in the mirror confirms for you.

If you really dislike how you look, then it may be that, as well as changing your attitude, you do need to consider changing your appearance.

What's stopping you?

So why don't you? We all know the overweight person whose 'diet starts tomorrow' and never visits a gym. The problem here may be that low self-esteem is affecting their effort rating as well. Or it may be that there are hidden benefits in not shaping up – the excuses it provides for general inadequacy, the lack of a relationship, etc.

Be honest with yourself

Ask yourself firmly whether any of these situations apply to you. Are you simply failing to acknowledge that there are areas in your life you need to deal with, by using the excuse that your wretched looks are the reason you can't do so? Think about this, and deal with it if necessary.

If you really do want to make changes, then set small, achievable goals and work towards them.

Activity
Set achievable goals

Use the table opposite to work out what changes you'd like to make, and how you could make them. This is a pro-active approach that should result in a feel-good factor from the effort and positive results.

Appearance changes I'd like to make
Physical characteristic I need to feel better about (e.g. flabby body):
What I need to do to improve this particular physical characteristic (e.g. firm up my physique and lose some weight):
Small, achievable goals (e.g. find out about nearest gym/how much it costs. If possible, make a decision to join. See a trainer about my problems and work out a programme. Ask for some dietary advice to go with the physical work out. Set a time limit for achieving my goal. Set a start date.):
Performance record (how am I doing?) (e.g. week 1 achievements, week 2 achievements – work within whatever goal timeframe you've set):

Simply making the decision to work on these issues should prove motivational and inspirational.

Cosmetic surgery

We'd neither recommend nor reject this as a possibility for you. We do recommend, however, that you work through the suggestions we've made before you start on this course. You may well decide that you feel good enough about yourself not to need it after all.

TOP TIP

♦ Low self-esteem can lead to 'not bothering' with ourselves, which, in turn, can manifest in poor body image. Make an effort to do all you can to improve your physical appearance. If you feel no better at all, you know at least that your problems lie in other, perhaps unexplored, areas.

BODY IMAGE

Refresh your memory

Before moving on, make sure that you're taking something helpful from this chapter with you. Write down the five most important points you've learned, or now have greater awareness of:

1 ....

2 ....

3 ....

4 ....

5 ....

Instant confidence booster

Use an affirmation.

Going out socially? Heading off for work? Worrying that your looks aren't up to scratch despite your efforts? Take a minute to say the following to yourself. 'I'm beautiful/handsome. Others find me attractive.'

Say this to yourself ten times, as soon as you can. Then, at various points throughout the day, repeat the process.

You'll be amazed by the power of your mind. You really will start to believe it (think how easily you're willing to believe negative suggestions).

Give it a go. It works! (And you can use it for anything.)

What's in your toolbox today?

You now have 28 skills in your toolbox. Review them and make sure that you're using at least some of them, where you have the chance to do so.

TOOLBOX
Items currently inside
28

BODY IMAGE

CHAPTER 9

BECOME AN OPTIMIST

'Do what you can, with what you have, where you are.'
Theodore Roosevelt, US President

> **Today you will learn ...**
>
> the beginnings of becoming an optimist – an excellent way to feel good about yourself.

Pessimistic thinking reinforces low self-esteem, while optimistic thinking allows us to be more self-accepting and retain a feel-good factor in the face of adversity.

Yet the only difference between an optimist and a pessimist is their thinking style. Nothing else. It's simply to do with how they perceive themselves and events around them, and the interpretations that they give to these perceptions.

For example, if your perception of yourself is that you're dull and uninteresting, your interpretation of possible interactions – 'and therefore no-one will like me' – is what cements your feel-bad factor.

An optimist might say, 'I think I came across as rather dull and uninteresting at the group talk yesterday' (i.e. the optimist's perception is specific rather than general) and the optimist's interpretation of that thought is more likely to be, 'Some people there may now have a poor impression, but many may not have noticed, and those who know me wouldn't have minded.'

As you learned earlier, feeling good about yourself has much more to do with your view of life than with your circumstances.

Increasing optimism

You already have the basic skills to achieve this. Having learned in Chapter 2 to recognise and then dispute negative, pessimistic thoughts, you can put this skill to excellent use in becoming a more optimistic thinker.

What do you think about the past? Do you consider that it determines your future? Do you feel that your genes and your upbringing determined your characteristics, and that you're therefore stuck with them? This type of belief will discourage you from making changes to your life, so take heart from the fact that change is possible, and that you'll manage it. Neither genes nor upbringing are as powerful as your mind.

Remember, an optimistic outlook is just down to your explanatory style, and nothing else. Tomorrow we'll look at simple changes you might make to your thinking style to develop your optimism.

TOP TIP

◆ An optimistic or pessimistic outlook comes from your (very changeable) thinking style – and nothing more.

Activity
What's your thinking style?

● Do you think that you'd feel better if you saw things in a more optimistic light?

● Think of two or three events coming up where the outcome is important but uncertain – for example, a sporting event you're taking part in or an appeal you've made against an unfair parking fine.

● Being completely honest with yourself, give yourself a rating between 1 and 10 (1 = totally pessimistic, 10 = totally optimistic) for the thoughts you have about the outcomes.

● Are the ratings fairly consistent? Does this give you a clue as to what type of thinking style you have?

BECOME AN OPTIMIST

Today you will learn ...

to start developing a more
optimistic thinking style.

There's no doubt about it – optimism is good for us. It's also a much nicer way to be, and the thoughts in our minds from moment to moment are more pleasant.

Take it seriously

It matters a great deal if your thinking is pessimistic. You're far more likely to suffer from depression and low self-esteem. You're more likely to give up easily in the face of setbacks. You're less likely to achieve success in the workplace because of lack of belief. It can affect your physical health as you'll suffer from stress more easily – and life is simply less fun.

Positive thinking

So how do optimists see things? What's so different? In his book, *Learned Optimism*, American psychologist Dr Martin Seligman identified what he calls three 'crucial dimensions' that determine the thinking styles of both pessimists and optimists. These are the three Ps – permanence, pervasiveness and personalisation. Let's look at the first 'P' now – the others will be covered over the next two days.

Permanence

If you tend to describe bad events that happen using words like 'always' and 'never', then you have a pessimistic thinking style. To think like an optimist, you need, instead, to use words like 'sometimes' and 'recently'. That's to say, the optimist sees setbacks as temporary, while the pessimist sees them as permanent. To illustrate the point, here are some examples.

BECOME AN OPTIMIST

The pessimist (permanent)	The optimist (temporary)
'I'll never learn to play the piano.'	'My piano lesson didn't go too well today.'
'Diets never work.'	'I'm finding it tough sticking to my diet during the Christmas period.'
'I'll never succeed in life.'	'My present job isn't doing me any favours.'

When something bad happens, many of us may feel distressed, even devastated, at the time. But for an optimistic thinker the distress lessens and then goes away, sometimes quite quickly. For the pessimist, it stays with them, even after only small setbacks. After a major setback, the pessimist may never recover. The thinking style doesn't allow the pessimist to see setbacks as temporary, from which they can recover, as an optimist does.

TOP TIP

◆ Start thinking like an optimist. When you have a setback, describe it to yourself in temporary, rather than permanent terms.

Activity
Challenge your pessimistic beliefs

Using the examples given above as a model, write down at least three beliefs that you have that are pessimistically permanent, for example, 'I'll never get slim'. Now write a 'temporary' explanation next to it. Practise this regularly to learn to think like an optimist.

BECOME AN OPTIMIST

The optimistic thinking style for explaining good events is the exact opposite of the thinking style for explaining bad events. An optimist will see good events that happen as permanent, whereas a pessimist will simply be waiting for them to come to an end. The table below gives some examples.

The pessimist (temporary)	The optimist (permanent)
'Good things never last.'	'There are many good things in my life.'
'The train's sure to be late today – it's been on time for two days running now.'	'It's great that the trains run on time these days.'
'Life is going too well – something has to go wrong soon'	'I love having my life on track at last.'

CASE STUDY

Jane and Tim both worked for the same company as graphic designers. When the company lost a major client, it was forced to make redundancies. Jane and Tim both lost their jobs. While both of them were devastated and their self-esteem was dented, Jane recovered far more quickly than Tim, and soon found alternative work. Tim, on the other hand, lost interest in everything, and put very little effort into applying for new jobs. These outcomes were due entirely to Jane and Tim's thinking styles. When they were made redundant, Jane's view was that her redundancy was a specific event that reflected the company's poor performance at the time. Tim's view was that his redundancy reflected his poor abilities as an employee and that he was obviously no good at anything.

BECOME AN OPTIMIST

Pervasiveness

When our thinking becomes pervasive, we move from the specific to the all-embracing. Instead of seeing one error as an isolated incident (as an optimist would) a pessimist sees the error as an indication of total incapability. In other words, they generalise the specific. Here are a few examples.

The pessimist (generalising)	The optimist (specific)
'I'm unattractive.'	'I'm unattractive to her.'
'I'm a hopeless driver.'	'I didn't drive well on the motorway today.
'Exercise machines are a waste of money.'	'This exercise machine doesn't perform as I'd hoped.'

⊙⤏ TOP TIP

◆ If you generalise the specific in your thinking, you lose self-esteem in a wide range of areas, rather than just the one area in which events failed to turn out well.

Be specific with your criticisms

● Think of some of the criticisms that your PFF has levelled at you. Write down at least three. Now see if you can write alongside a more specific explanation, using the examples above as a guide.

● Get used to being far more specific with any criticism of yourself or others. Stop using general statements. This is far kinder to yourself, fairer to others, more precise, and will help to raise your self-esteem.

BECOME AN OPTIMIST

Today you will learn ...

that de-personalising events will raise your self-esteem.

We've discussed the problems of personalisation on Day 30. Blaming ourselves for failure and taking things personally is a pessimist's viewpoint. An optimist will assess what's happened and apportion any blame in a more realistic way. For example, you do badly in an exam. A pessimist is more likely to blame themself for being a poor student, and possibly even give up a course as a result. An optimist will look at the bigger picture. How could you – thinking as an optimist – view this failure? Jot a few suggestions down below.

1 ....

2 ....

3 ....

Here are some possibilities:

◆ The tutor didn't explain it well.
◆ We had very little time to revise.
◆ The library was poorly stocked with the books we needed.
◆ I've heard that many students fail this particular exam.
◆ I didn't work as hard as I could have done – I'll need to put in more effort in future.
◆ I do find this subject difficult, but I did my best.

As a consequence of this, people who totally blame themselves for every failure will have low self-esteem. Learning not to personalise events but to look at the bigger picture will help you to think more optimistically and raise your self-esteem.

If you understand the principles of optimistic thinking, and apply the techniques you've learned to help you to challenge negative, pessimistic ideas and assumptions, you'll be on your way to becoming an optimist. Remember, optimists seldom have low self-esteem! You'll react to the normal setbacks of life much more positively, and bounce back from major disasters quickly, and well. You'll achieve more, generally, and – most importantly – you'll feel good about yourself.

TOP TIP

- ◆ Challenge negative, pessimistic thinking. Look at the bigger picture and broader possibilities to explain setbacks. Don't simply personalise them and blame yourself.

Activity
Take a broader view

- ● Think of the last setback you experienced where you felt you were partly or wholly to blame.

- ● What self-critical thoughts did you have?

- ● Using the example from these pages, write down at least four alternative or mitigating explanations for what happened. This can, of course, include your own contribution, but as a *part* of the whole situation, not the *total* situation.

- ● Review how you feel about the incident after you've done this. Is your self-esteem a little stronger from taking this broader view?

BECOME AN OPTIMIST

173

Refresh your memory

Before moving on, make sure that you're taking something helpful from this chapter with you. Write down the five most important points you've learned, or now have greater awareness of:

1 ....

2 ....

3 ....

4 ....

5 ....

Instant confidence booster

Act now! Start making holiday plans, arrange a family gathering, start searching the 'Situations vacant' columns for that new job, book a hairdressing appointment …

Getting motivated will boost your confidence and make you feel more excited about the future.

What's in your toolbox today?

No new skills in your toolbox right now, so it's an ideal time to run through the old ones and earmark those especially helpful to you.

TOOLBOX
Items currently inside
28

GET USEFUL POSITIVE
FEEDBACK

> **Today you will learn ...**
>
> that there's a value in input from others.

Total reliance on feedback from others is self-defeating, since it means that, if we're not getting praise and rewards to back up our own thinking, we lose confidence and retreat to the world of low self-esteem. This isn't to say we should discount it altogether. 'Other esteem' can be a valuable and helpful ally for several reasons.

The benefits of esteem from others

It helps to keep track of how you're doing

Getting esteem from others is an aide – a scorecard. It's input that tallies with our output. It helps us survive low periods when we find it hard to get self-motivated. Someone else paying us a compliment, congratulating us, even simply smiling and being friendly, can have a very positive lifting effect.

It makes you challenge your personal fault finder (PFF)

Another reason that 'other esteem' is extremely helpful is when our own view of ourselves is distorted. We tend to re-evaluate our opinions of ourselves when someone makes a comment that goes against our own thinking. For example, if you're giving yourself a hard time for being selfish and thoughtless, a friend commenting to you that you're always so kind and thoughtful makes you rethink your own position.

GET USEFUL POSITIVE FEEDBACK

It helps you to discover hidden qualities

'Other esteem' is helpful in that it can offer us insights into our positive qualities that we weren't even aware of. 'You always look so nice when you smile', 'You may not realise it, but your patience has made a real difference to me', 'How handy you are to do that so quickly.' Really? Qualities you had no idea about get pointed out to you and so help you to reassess your view of yourself.

TOP TIP

- Never depend on comments from others for your self-esteem, but accept it as a very helpful tool to keep your own perspective realistic rather than negative, and to learn to discover qualities you may not even have known about.

Activity

Assess positive comments from others

- How often in the past week (or longer, if necessary) have you had comments from anyone else that have been at odds with your worst view of yourself? These can be as simple as the post woman smiling at you or a neighbour waving.

- What negative view might this challenge? Your view that you're unlikeable? Or that you're not very approachable?

- Write as many cases down as you can think of.

- This is a good exercise to do on a regular – say, weekly – basis.

GET USEFUL POSITIVE FEEDBACK

Today you will learn ...

how to discover qualities you may not even have known that you had.

As we mentioned yesterday, one plus of 'other esteem' is that we can discover positive qualities about ourselves that we were unaware we had.

Activity

Pass on your admiration

In his book, *The Self-Esteem Workbook*, Glenn Shiraldi describes an activity you can do with your friends to help each of you discover more about your positive qualities. You can do this with just one or two people, but the more the merrier. You won't necessarily be able to do this immediately unless you have a houseful of people on tap, but agree to do it, either at work or at home, with the incentive that everybody who takes part will benefit!

Give each person a pen and sheet of paper. Write your own name at the top, and then pass the sheet to the person on your right. Each person then writes three points that they admire or appreciate about the person named on the sheet of paper, before passing it on to the next person, who does the same. Shiraldi suggests that you scatter your comments around the sheet, so that it's hard to identify who wrote what.

Once the lists have been completed by everyone, they're read out – your comments being read out by the person to your left, etc.

Don't!

When the comments are read out, don't devalue them by making deprecating remarks such as, 'What are you after?' or 'Obviously no-one is wearing glasses/knows what I'm really like', etc.

You're unique

When the comments are read out, you'll see that they're different for everyone, which adds to their value and genuineness. You may not have the same qualities as your best friend, but you both have a great amount to feel positive about.

Honesty and bonding

This is an excellent activity for families – especially if you have children (who can also suffer from low self-esteem, of course). Children are intrinsically honest and will feel over the moon to receive positive compliments. This exercise creates a real bond between the members of the group.

Your personalised emotional lift

Suggest that everyone keeps their own sheet of paper. They're excellent to refer back to at times when our PFF is on the march, and we could do with an emotional lift.

TOP TIP

◆ Accept that you have more positive qualities than you may be aware of. Many of them are only visible to others, because you either take them for granted or don't realise how attractive you appear when you, say, smile, or offer to help a friend.

GET USEFUL POSITIVE FEEDBACK

Refresh your memory

Before moving on, make sure that you're taking something helpful from this chapter with you. Write down the five most important points you've learned, or now have greater awareness of:

1 ....

2 ....

3 ....

4 ....

5 ....

Instant confidence booster

Start your day healthily. Instead of coffee, drink fruit juice. Then pick something delicious and nutritious for your breakfast, such as fruit, natural yoghurt, healthy cereal and low-fat milk.

Imagine each bite of food filling your whole body with energy. You'll want to keep things that way and you'll feel both virtuous and energised for the rest of the day. (In fact, try to keep it up for the day. You'll feel *really* good about yourself if you do that and it might be the start of a whole new you!)

What's in your toolbox at the moment?

We haven't added any more in this chapter – but would you like to? If there's anything you found especially helpful, pop it in the box.

TOOLBOX
Items currently inside
28

THE SKILLS OF
SOCIAL CONFIDENCE

For many people, specific situations cause their self-esteem to plummet, so we'll start to look now at skills that will help you to feel more confident in specific situations. As you practise these skills, your confidence will grow, and life will become much easier.

Do you lack confidence in social situations?

Social anxiety is one of the most common manifestations of low self-esteem. Many people with low self-esteem say that their PFF attacks them regularly when they're socialising. They feel exposed as being inadequate, an outsider, judged on their limited conversational abilities, appearance or level of confidence.

Do you avoid going out altogether?

For many people with low self-esteem, mixing socially can be such an ordeal that they avoid it altogether. This then makes it even more of an ordeal on the rare occasions that they can't duck out of an event.

Practise, practise, practise

Rule one of gaining social confidence is to practise! Once you've finished this book and learned the skills, you'll need to put yourself into as many social situations as you can, in order to use them.

Why is it so hard?

Is socialising an ordeal for you? Why is this? Think of at least five reasons your self-esteem takes a knock when you're with other people.

◆ Do you find it hard to think of something to say?
◆ Are you worried about the way you look?

THE SKILLS OF SOCIAL CONFIDENCE

◆ Do you think you come across as dull and boring?
◆ Do you get very anxious and blush?
◆ Do you feel like you're an outsider and not part of the group somehow?

What are your biggest concerns? List them below:

1 ....

2 ....

3 ....

4 ....

5 ....

Be reassured. Most people, if asked, would list many of the same difficulties. You're not alone. Appearing confident and being confident are quite different things. You'll learn to overcome these concerns with new skills – and to worry about them less as you relax more.

⊙⚡ TOP TIP

◆ Appreciate that social anxiety is a problem for many people. While you're busy worrying about your own weaknesses, the person you're talking to is probably having similar doubts and worries!

Activity
Work out your 'fear factor'

● Which social situations do you find most difficult? Write down half a dozen and rate them for their 'fear factor'. Do large gatherings unnerve you? Do you find meeting people you haven't met before an ordeal? Are one-to-one conversations unnerving? Are you more comfortable in work situations? In the pub?

● Then ask yourself, 'Why?' What's the most difficult aspect of these situations for you?

THE SKILLS OF SOCIAL CONFIDENCE

Today you will learn ...

how easy or difficult you find it to socialise.

Do this quiz to see how easy or difficult you find it to make friends and keep a social circle.

Activity

Social confidence quiz

Rate each answer from 1 to 10 according to your level of agreement/disagreement.

1 Do you find it difficult to approach others, say, at a party, with people you don't know well? (1 = difficult, 10 = easy)

2 Do you think you're open and easy to talk to, or closed and rather distant? (1 = closed, 10 = open)

3 How approachable do you consider you are to others? (1 = not at all, 10 = very)

4 Do you find yourself feeling lonely, even in a room full of people? (1 = very often, 10 = never)

5 Do you find it difficult to let other people know how you're feeling, especially if you're worried or unhappy? (1 = difficult, 10 = easy)

6 Are other people inclined to tell you their problems? (1 = rarely, 10 = often)

7 In a group of friends, do you feel that you have little to say compared to others? (1 = always, 10 = never)

THE SKILLS OF SOCIAL CONFIDENCE

8 Do you spend much of your time with others worrying about how you come across, how you look, what they might be thinking about you generally? (1 = very much, 10 = not at all)

9 Would you normally prefer to stay home than go to a function where you don't know anybody (even though it would be a good event)? (1 = every time, 10 = no, I'd always go)

10 Have you ever suffered from feelings of panic or high anxiety when going into a room full of people? (1 = often, 10 = never)

Your total score

80–100: Skip this chapter!
50–80: You're fairly normal. But your self-esteem will benefit from practising new skills.
30–50: You find socialising and making friends difficult.
Less than 30: Your self-esteem is almost certainly keeping you isolated and stopping you from mixing or making friends.

Of the questions asked, on which three was your score the lowest? Which three the highest? Your answers will give you insight into the areas you need to work on the most – from reducing anxiety to learning how to listen better, for example.

TOP TIP

◆ Our personal fault finder always has a field day in social situations. This is normal, and no matter how hard you find social situations now, you can make huge strides in becoming more confident.

THE SKILLS OF SOCIAL CONFIDENCE

Today you will learn ...

how to make a good first
impression.

Many of us want people to like us when they meet us. That's natural. So before we even open our mouths (and, for many of us, feel that we 'blow it') it's worth having an overview of what's appealing – and unappealing.

Psychotherapist Christine Webber conducted a survey in 2002 in which she asked people what they looked for especially when they met someone for the first time. From the responses, she constructed a list of the top 15 turn-ons and turn-offs.

We like ...

◆ Sense of humour
◆ Enthusiasm
◆ Friendliness
◆ Good eye contact
◆ Nice smile and pleasant facial expression
◆ Interest in the person you're talking to
◆ Chatty
◆ Good listener
◆ Genuine
◆ Mutual interests
◆ Nice looking
◆ Intelligent
◆ Polite
◆ Smells nice
◆ Good dress sense

What we don't like ...

◆ Over-confidence
◆ Lack of interest
◆ Insincerity
◆ Arrogance
◆ Rudeness
◆ Poor eye contact
◆ Poor personal hygiene
◆ Loudness
◆ Being a bore
◆ Being too serious
◆ Lack of friendliness
◆ Aggressiveness
◆ Narrow-mindedness
◆ Appearance of not being bothered
◆ Poor or inappropriate dress sense

These lists have been rated in order of importance – so you can see that a sense of humour and friendliness is rated as much more valuable to those you meet than what you're wearing or how intelligent you are. Notice these points – they'll give you a head start on increasing your self-esteem.

SKILL FOR YOUR
TOOLBOX
29

Far too many of us believe we're judged negatively on things that aren't very important to others.

You may say, 'But many of these qualities don't come naturally to me.' This isn't necessarily true, but we'll work with you on them now – you'll only be honing skills you already have, but which you don't believe you have, so therefore use only rarely. Let's get them out and brush them up.!

 TOP TIP

♦ Don't be too hard on yourself – warmth and interest are the key skills you need socially. Don't agonise over your hairstyle or knowledge of current affairs.

Activity
Focus on the turn-ons!

Re-read the list of turn-ons above. Do you think that you already have any of these qualities? If so, how many? (More than you thought?) Do the same for the turn-offs. Do you have perhaps less than you thought?

What quality would you most like to possess to increase your social confidence? Where does that feature on the list above? Is there anything here you can improve on?

THE SKILLS OF SOCIAL CONFIDENCE

When low self-esteem kicks in socially, do any of the following thoughts sound familiar?

Today you will learn ...

what hampers your social confidence.

◆ You feel you're in the lime-light, being judged by others.
◆ You feel you need to impress people if they're to like you.
◆ You believe you have to put on a front, so that people don't discover the 'real' you.
◆ You feel inferior and defective in comparison with others.
◆ You feel that you can read the minds of people you're talking to.
◆ You dread not knowing what to say next and making a fool of yourself.

Do any (or many) of these statements have a familiar ring to you? Do these thoughts and ideas come into your mind regularly when you're mixing with others?

Here's a question ... what do all the above statements have in common?

Any suggestions? Write something down (which can't be, 'I don't know'!)

....

We hope you've written:

'These thoughts are all about *me*.'

Here you are, in a social situation with the chance to learn and discover quite a bit about the people you're with, and what are you doing?

Just thinking about yourself!

Don't worry, this is quite natural – but you need to put a stop to it.

THE SKILLS OF SOCIAL CONFIDENCE

Parallel thought processes

When we're attempting to listen to what someone else is saying at the same time as constantly thinking about ourselves – and the impression we're creating – this is called 'parallel thought processes'. As you can imagine, running two sets of parallel thoughts at once is very difficult. So what happens? Instead of focusing on the person we're talking to, we focus on ourselves. We become so absorbed in what we'll say when they stop talking, whether what we previously said was silly, what they think of our hair style, general presentation, tone of voice, etc. that we totally forget to LISTEN! No wonder we come across as looking a little bland and uninterested. No wonder we don't know what to say when the other person stops talking. No wonder we feel rather inadequate.

SKILL FOR YOUR
TOOLBOX
30

Turn the 'self-talk switch' off!

TOP TIP

◆   Realise that being overly self-absorbed is the most damaging aspect of poor social skills. It prevents us from focusing on others and means we come across poorly. Turn the parallel thought switch off.

Activity

Check out your thought processes

Imagine yourself in a social group, talking to someone you've never met before. What are the likeliest thoughts going through your mind? Jot them down. Are they all thoughts about you? Do you think they might prevent you from focusing properly on the other person? These are your parallel thought processes. Become much more aware of them.

THE SKILLS OF SOCIAL CONFIDENCE

'You gain strength, courage, and confidence by every experience in which you really stop and look fear in the face.' Eleanor Roosevelt, wife of former US President

Today you will learn ...

to say 'boo' to the goose and get that conversational ball rolling.

Social shyness can make it very difficult to get into a conversation. Silence is awkward and you desperately wish that someone would say *something* to get the ball rolling.

CASE STUDY

Peter worked in a busy office as an IT expert. He was good at his job, which involved a lot of talking – but only to computers.

When Peter went the coffee machine, he passed three colleagues without saying a word to them. At the machine, there were a couple of staff members chatting to each other as they chose their drink. They glanced at Peter and smiled, but still, Peter didn't say anything.

Peter thought, 'No-one ever talks to me. I guess they think I'm just a boring computer nerd. If someone just said something, I think I'd get some confidence, but they just walk on by ...'

Why did Peter have no trouble 'conversing' with his computers, yet lots of trouble conversing with people? What's the one thing that Peter's computers didn't do, that he feels human beings do?

He feels that people *judge* him negatively, and that's why they don't start conversations.

Do you ever feel like this? Do you wish people would be chattier, friendlier, show you that you're 'one of them', 'part of the group', 'a valued team member'? If so, stop wishing and make it happen!

Strike up a conversation

You're going to start the conversation. You're going to say *one sentence* to at least three people today *whom you have no reason to speak to.* When you see the postman/woman walk by, say, 'Nice weather today' (or something similar) – and see how they respond. When your neighbour leaves their home at the same time as you do, make a simple, friendly comment such as, 'I like your coat!' When you buy something in a shop, have a word to the cashier, 'You're busy today' or the person behind you in the queue, 'I see you prefer blue ones …'.

Then, most importantly, see what response you get (don't worry about the odd rebuff – everyone gets those sometimes).

TOP TIP

♦ Practise in small ways with people where it doesn't really matter much how things go, then you'll eventually be able to say 'boo' to every goose out there!

Activity Practise starting conversations

Practise the type of mini-conversations suggested above with at least three people.

● Say *one* positive comment to each person.

● How did they respond?

● What happened next?

● How did you feel afterwards?

> ### Today you will learn ...
>
> that gaining social confidence
> is easier than you think.

You can now improve on other social skills. What do you think the most important skill might be?

Not sure? Think about turning the parallel thought switch off. What are you left with?

Active listening

This will turn you into the most popular person on the social circuit. It has nothing to do with being witty, clever and well dressed, and everything to do with being genuinely interested in other people.

SKILL FOR YOUR
TOOLBOX
31

What do you think the skills of active listening might be?

Eye contact

Hold eye contact with the other person. This doesn't mean staring fixedly at them, but rather engaging with them – showing them your interest in them rather than letting your eyes roam round the room.

Focus

You won't need to talk very much, but it really helps if you can listen attentively. This is why you need to turn off your self-thoughts so that you focus on what the other person is saying – which will not *necessarily* be fascinating, although it helps!

'Tell me more'

Engrave this on the back of your hand! You won't need to have many more conversational skills than this one phrase. Most people will be only too delighted to tell you more if you're creating a feeling of real interest in what they're saying.

Pick a word

When 'tell me more' isn't quite appropriate, or already over-used, the simplest skill is to pick a word from the last sentence spoken and ask a question about that. If, for example, someone is talking about a holiday they recently had Istanbul, you have the opportunity to say something like, 'Istanbul. I've never been there. What's it like?' or use the word 'holiday' to ask, 'Was that your first/only holiday this year? Where else have you been?'

Open questions

Make sure you don't ask questions where monosyllabic 'yes' or 'no' are possible answers. Perhaps ask for an opinion instead.

Practise

Now use this skill. Talk to new people every day. Speak to the bus driver, the supermarket assistant – people you may not have bothered with before. Simply get used to being social – you'll be delighted with the response.

It's easy once you know how!

⊙⊶ TOP TIP

- ◆ Become an active listener. This is your key to social confidence.

Activity
Practise active listening

Start practising active listening. You may need to create a situation, but have a go, using the skills discussed above. Get used to it. Then keep practising regularly.

THE SKILLS OF SOCIAL CONFIDENCE

Refresh your memory

Before moving on, make sure that you're taking something helpful from this chapter with you. Write down the five most important points you've learned, or now have greater awareness of:

1 ....

2 ....

3 ....

4 ....

5 ....

Instant confidence booster

Go out right now (or as soon as practical) and take some exercise. A good, vigorous, half-hour walk will do. Then vow to keep it up. Your self-esteem will rocket when you know that you feel fit and healthy and can cope with life's demands. Exercise also helps your brain to manufacture more 'feel good' chemicals, which will lift your mood even more and increase your self-esteem.

What's in your toolbox?

You now have 31 skills in your toolbox. Review them and make sure that you're using at least some of them, where you have the chance to do so.

TOOLBOX
Items currently inside
31

CHAPTER 12

SELF-ESTEEM IN RELATIONSHIPS

> **Today you will learn ...**
>
> to take a look at why finding or keeping a good relationship may be difficult for you.

A major area of our lives that can be affected by our low self-esteem is that of relationships. We may feel friendless, and/or we may have difficulty in finding or holding on to romantic love.

At the bottom of these difficulties lie our own feelings of inadequacy: 'I'm not especially loveable/like-able, so why would anyone really care about me?'

We're not attempting to simplify the many complex problems that exist in relationships, but are focusing solely on issues of self-esteem.

Quick quiz

Answer the questions below, and tick any that apply to you.

1 Are you in a relationship that you worry about? ☐

2 Would you like to be in a relationship, but feel that you don't have enough to offer? ☐

3 Do you accept sub-standard relationships because you feel you're not worth a good one? ☐

4 Are you waiting for your partner to 'find you out' and see that you're really not worth loving? ☐

5 Do you tend to 'hold back' in relationships so that your partner doesn't discover all your faults and weakness? ☐

6 Do you actively avoid relationships because you can't conceive of yourself as loveable? ☐

7 Do you tend to sabotage perfectly good relationships on the basis that it will all end in tears at some point, so better now than later? ☐

8 Do you spoil relationships by being very needy? ☐

9 Do you pick arguments simply to rouse your partner to show that he or she 'really cares'? ☐

10 Do you feel despondent wondering whether you'll ever feel really loved and content? ☐

Unfortunately, if you ticked even one of these statements, your self-esteem is sabotaging your relationship chances. Confidence in relationships only comes from confidence in ourselves. We need to learn to like ourselves first.

A common problem is that, where our self-esteem is low, we look for someone else to make us feel better. We decide that if we're liked and loved by others, then we'll like and love ourselves.

This thinking error is what leads to relationship failure. If we don't like ourselves, why would we expect others to like us?

SKILL FOR YOUR
TOOLBOX
32

In the previous chapter we discussed being a good listener. The secret of finding and retaining a good relationship is very similar. We need to stop thinking and worrying about ourselves, and develop more of a focus on others.

TOP TIP

♦ We need to love ourselves if we want others to love us as well. In relationship terms, this means offering something, rather than simply hoping to take something from a friendship or romance.

Activity
What's holding you back in relationships?

What do you believe prevents you from finding or retaining a happy relationship? Write your answers down. Do the answers relate more to faults you feel you have that make you unlovable, or do they relate more to faults in most people you meet that make *them* unlovable?

SELF-ESTEEM IN RELATIONSHIPS

Today you will learn ...

to take a look at why finding or
keeping a good relationship
may be difficult for you.

Many people say that they have
difficulty finding a relationship.
This can be because we expect too
much of other people – especially
if we're going to need them to
enhance our self-esteem. They're
going to need to be pretty special
to be able to do that for us.

SKILL FOR YOUR
TOOLBOX
33

Change your thinking on this, and do
the following.

Take a real interest in people you meet

This is an excellent skill for self-esteem. Building on the work in the
last chapter, you're basically 'off-focusing'. Instead of thinking about
yourself, *your* needs, *your* inadequacies, you focus on who you are with
and ensure you find out about *them*.

This exercise will help you build confidence in how likeable you are,
and is very good practise for relationship-building.

Good communication

When we communicate well
with friends or our partners, we
feel confident and good about
ourselves. Poor communication
can make us angry and upset, or
fuels feelings of inadequacy.

In your closest relationships it
means – yet again – listening well.

When we're in very intimate relationships, and no longer on 'best behaviour', we spend a great deal of time either talking or waiting. We're either saying our piece, or waiting for our partner to finish speaking so that we can say our next piece. We don't actively listen.

Understanding

Communicating well with your partner will give you confidence. You'll communicate well if you first listen to what they have to say (rather than believing that what you have to say is more important) and then ensuring that you've understood it by commenting in a constructive way.

If James tells Mary that he's unhappy about the fact that she doesn't like him spending time in the pub with his friends, it's best for her not to respond with a statement such as, 'You obviously prefer being there rather than here with me', but to try to understand what he's saying, and express how she feels – so that James is given the opportunity to find a solution. For example, 'I appreciate that you like to relax after work with your friends sometimes, but I miss you as well. How can we resolve this?'

TOP TIP

- Showing interest, and communicating well through listening and understanding, will kick-start new relationships, enhance those you already have, and give you lots of confidence.

Activity
Listen more

With everyone you come into contact with today, either at work, at home or socially, speak less and listen more. Be aware of the outcomes. How do you feel about yourself and what's your perception of how others view you when you do this?

SELF-ESTEEM IN RELATIONSHIPS

Today you will learn ...

to raise your own self-esteem rather than seek it from your partner.

Just be nice! How simple is that?! Too simple for you?

Let's explain it this way. One of the difficulties in relationships is our high expectations. The lower our self-esteem the higher our expectations are. We 'need' our partner to do all the right things, to notice if we're unhappy, to buy the right birthday present, to spot our new haircut or the weight we've lost – in other words, we need *them* to make *us* feel good about ourselves.

The result of these demands can be disappointment, and disappointment will confirm our worst fears – we've either made a bad choice of partner, or we're not worth treating lovingly and well.

Where's the focus here? Yes, we're back chasing self-esteem again. Looking for it from our relationship, failing to find it, becoming distressed, feeling worse ... Once again, we've become totally self-focused. It's all about *us* again.

'The secret of a good relationship isn't finding the right person, but *being* the right person.' Anon

TOP TIP

- Learn to get confidence through kindness rather than neediness. You don't have to get it back all the time in order to feel good.

Activity Stop being needy

For two days – for a start – stop being needy. Stop seeing issues in your terms, and think only about what you can do for your partner. This isn't being a wimp: it's a genuine exercise in discovering whether you can feel better about yourself by behaving nicely rather than in a needy way.

At the end of the two days, ask yourself the following questions:

1 How do I feel about myself and my behaviour (irrespective of the responses I got)?

2 Do I feel better about myself – have I given it my best, even in adverse circumstances?

3 Have I noticed any change in my partner? Has he or she appreciated my behaviour or taken it for granted?

4 Would I feel better if I carried on making an effort like this?

5 How might this affect my self-esteem?

You may say that you have a tricky partner who doesn't deserve to be at the receiving end of your nice behaviour, and will take you – and nice behaviour – for granted. Sadly, it's not the remit of this book to deal with difficult relationships, and you may have to make your own decisions here or find help elsewhere. We're attempting to help you find ways to increase your own self-esteem within your relationship – even if this eventually encourages you to have the confidence to leave a relationship that's unhealthy and unrewarding.

Resolve to do a further two days of giving if you can – and then more, and more, as you cement your confidence and you get back what you give.

SELF-ESTEEM IN RELATIONSHIPS

When our self-esteem is low, it's easy to sabotage relationships with defeatist behaviour. This can include assuming the worst, focusing on the negative, not allowing yourself to feel exposed in case you get hurt – the type of behaviour that means our partner never really gets to know the real person behind this smoke screen.

To succeed in dislodging low self-esteem in *any* area of your life, you need to risk a bit. You need to stretch yourself a little, change defeatist behaviours, do something new without being certain of the outcome. It's no different with intimate relationships. A wonderful saying is; 'To risk nothing is to risk everything.'

Yes, you might get hurt if a relationship goes wrong – but you'll cope, and can save your energies to deal with that if it happens. Don't waste your energies on it now. You need to risk being open, speaking from your heart, letting your partner know the real you.

Think about the following:

1 With whom do I feel most at ease? a) Someone who tells me only 'the good stuff' about themselves and their life? Or b) The person who is open with me about their faults and weaknesses?
2 If I chose b), why?
3 If I chose b), do I like them more or less now they've confided in me?
4 Do I feel more comfortable with someone who's self-effacing – willing to laugh at themselves and admit their mistakes, or do I prefer someone who never makes mistakes?
5 Do I appreciate someone who's willing to tell me intimate details about their life or do I prefer not to know?
6 Do I feel flattered that someone sees me as someone they can tell these things to?

7 Based on the above, if I reverse the positions, and I become the open, honest, intimate-detail-revealing risk-taker, is my partner likely to feel more loving and at ease with me or less?

SKILL FOR YOUR TOOLBOX 34

Remember, to risk nothing is to risk everything. Take a risk with openness and honesty. The boost it will give your confidence to discover how much more you're loved, rather than how much less you're loved, will be well worth it.

TOP TIP

◆ Take the risk of being open and honest in your relationships. Your self-esteem will increase, not decrease, and your relationship will develop positively.

Risk opening up to people

● Every day this week, tell someone close to you – your partner if you have one, your best friend, a work colleague – one aspect about yourself that they didn't know before.

● Be aware of how easy or difficult you found that, and any significant response from the person you told.

● Build upon being more open into your daily life, until you feel quite comfortable and confident doing it.

SELF-ESTEEM IN RELATIONSHIPS

> **Today you will learn ...**
>
> to hold your head up high when relationships go wrong.

When a relationship ends, and it's not our choice, it can have the most devastating effect on our self-esteem. The pain of losing someone we love is heartbreaking, and any extra pain caused by feelings of worthlessness and unlovability can be exremely hard to bear.

In some cases, people vow never to put themselves through these terrible emotions again. They see the ending as a sign that they're not worthy of being loved and that this is how things would end again.

While accepting heartbreak, don't allow your self-worth to be called into question.

'We are never so helplessly unhappy as when we lose love.'
Sigmund Freud, creator of Analytical Therapy and author

Use your thinking skills

One of the most important things is not to generalise the specific. This *particular* relationship didn't work out. This *particular* person turned out not to be right for you. This doesn't mean you're unlovable. Use your evidence finding skills ...

◆ Have you ever been loved before?
◆ Who else has loved you in your life?
◆ What does this mean about your lovability?

Behave with dignity

If you can keep your dignity, not matter how your heart is breaking, you'll keep your self-esteem. Do the following:

◆ Don't say too much to the person you're splitting up with. It's easy to want to apportion blame, go into detail about misunderstandings, how you feel, what happened when, etc. Don't do this. It's too much information, will not be heard, and will not make any *difference*. Say as little as possible, and you may be respected for this – and you'll respect yourself.

◆ If you still love the person, tell them so, but with grace and dignity, and without asking anything in return.

◆ Determine not to contact them, not to beg or plead or behave in any way that you may regret later and will cause you more pain and regret. You have more chance that your lost love will contact you at some point if they hear nothing from you (if that's what you want, of course).

◆ Be certain that, however much your heart is breaking, you've done nothing wrong and can hold your head up high. The difference this type of dignity will make to your self-esteem in the aftermath will be quite spectacular.

TOP TIP

◆ You can't always keep the person you loved, but you can keep your self-esteem if you act with dignity.

Activity

Has this happened before?

● If you've found yourself in this situation in the past, look back at how you dealt with it. What lowered your self-esteem the most?

● If it was to do with your own behaviour, what could you learn from that?

SELF-ESTEEM IN RELATIONSHIPS

Refresh your memory

Before moving on, make sure that you're taking something helpful from this chapter with you. Write down the five most important points you've learned, or now have greater awareness of:

1 ....

2 ....

3 ....

4 ....

5 ....

Instant confidence booster

For instant relationship confidence, here are two things to do as soon as you get a chance:

1 Stay cool and relaxed over something you could (rightfully) gripe about.

2 Say, 'No thank you', instead of always saying, 'Yes', if it's something you really aren't sure about.

You'll gain the respect of your partner for both of these things, and you'll feel good about yourself.

So what's in your toolbox?

You now have 34 skills in your toolbox. Review them and make sure that you're using at least some of them, where you have the chance to do so.

TOOLBOX
Items currently inside
34

CHAPTER 13

DEVELOPING AS A
PERSON TO INCREASE
SELF-ESTEEM

'When you've gone so far that you can't manage one more step,
then you've gone just half the distance that you're capable of.'
Greenland proverb

> **Today you will learn ...**
>
> to begin developing values that
> create good self-esteem.

Finding true happiness

Over the years, psychologists worldwide have conducted a great deal of research to pinpoint the most important values we humans either have, or need to develop, in order to feel truly happy and contented. Let's consider some of those that get flagged up again and again as making a huge difference to people's lives.

If you do your best to incorporate these values into your daily life, your feel-good factor will rise up off the chart. Your life will flourish and you'll reach your highest potential.

Negative thoughts give you valuable information

If you still suffer from a variety of negative thoughts and emotions, don't worry. These are giving you valuable information about the areas in which you can make changes. If you feel gloomy and sad, then you need to focus on developing the value of *cheerfulness*. If life seems flat and dreary, then you can learn to build *passion* into your life. If you feel inadequate and unable to achieve your goals, then some *determination* will make a difference.

Making a contribution

SKILL FOR YOUR
TOOLBOX
35

If you can consistently develop the idea of contributing to others' well-being, the sense of pride and self-esteem you'll feel will be more than any wealth, celebrity or accomplishment can ever offer.

In his book *Authentic Happiness*, Martin Seligman relates how he gave a class of students an assignment that involved doing one altruistic act (doing something for others, with no expectation of personal reward), and one pleasurable thing, every day for a week. He asked them to rate the feel-good factor that they got from these things. He discovered that, while initially, the feel-good factor for both pleasurable and altruistic things was similar, over the following week, when the exercise was over, the feel-good factor for the altruistic acts remained far higher than that for the pleasurable acts.

Not only does altruism raise your self-esteem (and rightly so), but the positive feel-good feelings will stay with you, rather than fade away.

TOP TIP

♦ Developing core values that help you to feel good about yourself will ensure that your self-esteem becomes healthy and enduring.

Activity **Be altruistic**

● Give Martin Seligman's experiment a go for a week. In a small way, either at work or at home, make sure that you do one pleasurable thing and one altruistic thing on a daily basis.

● Rate the feel-good factor (1 = OK, 10 = very high). Note down your ratings.

● Go back to your ratings a week later. Rate the feel-good factors again. Which acts still give you the highest rating?

DEVELOPING AS A PERSON TO INCREASE SELF-ESTEEM

'One of the most difficult things to give away is kindness, for it's usually returned.' Mark Ortman, author

What are the values that guide your life? Are there values you wish you had but don't feel that you've got? If not, why not?

Today you will learn ...

more about the values that you can develop to increase your self-esteem.

Activity

What are your values?

In your notebook, list the core values that are meaningful to you, and which you consider would enhance your self-esteem. A good way of working this out is to pick someone whom you admire for their character (rather than skills or abilities) and write down what qualities you think they possess that make them an admirable person.

Here are some suggestions:

◆ Love and warmth
◆ Humour and cheerfulness
◆ Kindness
◆ Vitality
◆ Gratitude
◆ Humility
◆ Forgiveness
◆ Integrity
◆ Excitement and passion
◆ Determination
◆ Flexibility.

SKILL FOR YOUR
TOOLBOX
36

Your task is to select which of these attributes are important to you, and to make a real effort to develop them and to incorporate them into your life. We are going to look at each in turn.

Determination

This is an attribute that you must possess or develop if you're going to create lasting self-esteem for yourself. Determination will help you to meet challenges and overcome setbacks. It's what will make the difference between feeling totally stuck, and moving forwards powerfully and confidently.

Love and warmth

You can develop these qualities by using many of the skills you've already worked on – most importantly, focusing on others rather than yourself. Stop seeing everything as being about you, and become genuinely interested in and caring of other people and their problems and situations. Ask yourself what you could do to help, even if it's nothing more than listening, or being available. Don't always respond to anger with anger – see if you can melt the anger by responding with warmth and compassion. This isn't weakness, it's strength (and therefore, quite hard to do).

Appreciation and gratitude

Take a minute to stop thinking about what you don't have, and then think about what you do have. Concentrate on appreciating all the good things that have come into your life, the helpful things that people have done for you and the joy of what you've achieved. You'll enhance your life greatly by thinking in this more appreciative way.

 TOP TIP

♦ Work out which basic, self-esteem-increasing values you may already have (but have failed to focus on) or would like to develop. This will give you a focus as you move forward.

DEVELOPING AS A PERSON TO INCREASE SELF-ESTEEM

Today you will learn ...

about more core qualities you may want to develop – and learn why they're worth developing.

Forgiveness

When we fail to forgive people, we're the ones who remain disturbed and upset, and we let this affect other areas of our lives. Taking a 'Why should I?/How could they?' approach is all very well, but you're the one who'll remain resentful and bitter. How does this help you? Forgiving is what allows us to move on. It creates respect from others and gives us self-respect. It's worth working on.

Humour and cheerfulness

These are very visible qualities. Are they necessary? Yes, they are! Being happy within yourself, but not sharing it with others, is only half of a good thing. Being overtly cheerful will make the people around you happier as well. Think of it this way. When things are tough, doesn't being cheerful make things any better?

Humility and integrity

See yourself as neither inferior nor superior to anyone else. Treat others in this same way. Have respect for the simple person; don't be in awe of the powerful person. Do your best at all times without looking for praise or reward.

Excitement, passion and vitality

These are qualities you can bring into your life quite quietly. They don't have to involve being a noisy extrovert or bubbling with ideas (although they can), but rather, they encourage you to think pro-actively and get moving! You can't be excited and passionate if you're slumped in a chair listening to your PFF having a go at you.

Flexibility

Flexibility as a value? Yes. It's one that will almost guarantee feeling good. Consider the thinking skills you've learned. These could also be called 'learning to think flexibly' or, 'if your approach isn't working, change your approach'. Being flexible is about being willing to change your rules for living, your assumptions, the personal meaning you attach to life and your actions. Throughout your life there will be situations you're not able to control, so adopting a flexible approach to what these events mean will enable you to feel good about yourself.

TOP TIP

♦ Learn to focus much more on developing basic qualities, rather than despairing over your weaknesses. If you do this, your weaknesses may disappear, or you may view them in a less critical light.

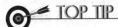

What qualities do you already have?

Read through today and Day 93 again. Do a self-audit based on which, if any, of these qualities you think you already have. If you've not already written them down, do so now, and then rate them, according to how strongly you believe you already have them. For example, if you feel you're already fairly cheerful, or normally forgiving, rate this quality from 0 per cent = not at all, to 100 per cent = totally. Rating is important to allow you to further develop qualities you already possess, and to measure future improvement.

DEVELOPING AS A PERSON TO INCREASE SELF-ESTEEM

Today you will learn ...

to plan the development of your own values.

We hope that you now have an idea of the personal values that you'd like to improve or possess. Within the scope of this book it's impossible to work in detail with you on each of these values, but we can help you to develop a plan to work on yourself on an on-going basis.

It's also a good idea to read more about these values. Have a go at, *The Art of Happiness* by H.E. The Dalai Lama, *Authentic Happiness* by Martin Seligman, or *The Seven Habits of Highly Successful People* by Steven Covey. Each of these books discusses in depth how to acquire the basic core values that have been identified throughout history, across nations and different religious beliefs to be those that will bring us lasting happiness.

SKILL FOR YOUR TOOLBOX 37

Now start work on developing your personal plan. You can build on it over days, weeks and months to enhance your own core values, and/or help you to master new ones. First, fill in the overview. This will help to clarify where you are now and what you need to work on. After four weeks of work, you can re-evaluate what improvements you've made, and assess what you need to do further.

TOP TIP

◆ Your self-esteem will increase as you work on your values. Take the time to do some extra reading so that you understand them in greater depth.

Activity

Fill in your personal plan overview

Copy and complete the table below.

Developing values – my personal plan overview

Value(s) that I'd like to develop/develop further.

Do I have elements of these values now? List any that you do.

Rate how strongly you feel you currently have each value (0 per cent = not at all, 100 per cent = totally)

At the end of four weeks, after working on them, how have my present values improved, and what new values do I now have? Rate them now. Has the rating improved?

What further work do I need to do? (For example, do I need to record how I'm doing for another four weeks? Are there certain opportunities I'm not taking? Do I care more about some values than others?)

> **Today you will learn ...**
>
> to practise your new values on
> a regular basis.

Once you've filled in the overview from Day 95, use the 'Personal plan weekly log' on page 233 on a weekly basis for four weeks.

One at a time

Work on one new value at a time. In week 2 you can build in a second value, while carrying on with the first, and in week 3, a third value, and so on. You'll need to make sure that you do achieve these values, even if this means putting in extra effort as you introduce new behaviours and ways of being that will reflect them.

Second nature

After four weeks, you may find that the values are starting to become second nature. If you're still struggling, then continue with this written exercise for a further four weeks – or as long as it takes for you to feel that they're a more natural part of you.

Make changes if you need to

You're free to make changes as you go along. You'll only be able to measure your improved feel-good factor as you act new behaviours out. Some may surprise you – for example, you might start doing more for others reluctantly, only to discover that your feel-good rating is much higher than you'd predicted. Equally, you may set great store by being flexible, only to find that, unless you're careful, you're simply 'giving in' to things too easily. Redefine your values in the light of what you discover as you work on them.

TOP TIP

- One popular viewpoint is that something becomes a habit after 21 days. With a further seven 'to spare', you can feel quite confident that you'll master the values that will increase your self-esteem in four weeks.

Activity

Start your weekly log

Make a start on your weekly log. This is set out on page 233 (you may wish to make some copies). Decide where you'll keep it so that it's available to you when you need to make any notes in it. Promise yourself that you'll keep this log on a regular basis for at least a month.

DEVELOPING AS A PERSON TO INCREASE SELF-ESTEEM

Today you will learn ...

how to recover from the irrecoverable.

Low self-esteem isn't always simply an error of thinking. It can sometimes be caused by a serious error of judgement.

Sometimes in our lives we make mistakes that have serious consequences and are hard to live with – and the resulting guilt and shame can leave us not knowing how to recover.

We can recover

If we behaved in a bad or stupid way in the past, this doesn't mean that we're a bad or stupid person through and through. It's simply evidence that we're fallible. We can learn from such experiences and perhaps become even better people in the future in our desire to actively change our lives.

⊙✎ TOP TIP

♦ Making bad decisions in the past doesn't prevent us from becoming better people in the future and making meaningful and significant contributions to the lives of ourselves and others.

Activity Revisit your past mistakes

Only do this exercise if this particular cause of low self-esteem applies to you. If you suffer from feelings of worthlessness due to past mistakes or decisions, painful though this will be, revisit them now, and write them down if you can. Keep them by you as you read Day 98, where you'll learn skills to deal with them. (If you think this activity will be overwhelming then, of course, you don't have to do it.)

CASE STUDY

Peter worked at an ambulance call centre, responsible for answering incoming calls and prioritising them, so that ambulances were always immediately on the scene for the most serious incidents first.

One day, Peter received two calls at the same time that seemed equally serious. But he only had one ambulance immediately available and he had to make a decision as to where to send it. Soon after he made his decision, Peter felt that it had perhaps been the wrong one and became quite traumatised by this thought. He kept going over whether somebody hadn't received the best care because of the choice he'd been forced to make. Following this incident, Peter found it harder and harder to continue with the job, and eventually handed in his notice.

Peter kept wondering whether he'd made other wrong decisions. His sense of guilt at what he might have done wouldn't leave him and he found it hard to feel good about himself again.

Then a friend who was worried about Peter suggested that, although Peter couldn't undo the past, he could use his experience to help others in the future. As a result, Peter joined the Samaritans, and started helping those who felt who were desperate and were finding it hard to live. This enabled him to make a real contribution to the lives of others. It also helped him to realise that we all make (or believe we may have made) bad decisions sometimes, but that doesn't mean we don't have integrity or value.

DEVELOPING AS A PERSON TO INCREASE SELF-ESTEEM

DAY 98: RECOVERY FROM GUILT AND SHAME

> **Today you will learn ...**
>
> skills to help you to tackle guilt and shame.

Three important questions to ask yourself to help you move forward when bad events happen for which you feel you were to blame, are:

- 'What can I learn from this?'
- 'In what way am I stronger as a result of this experience?'
- 'What can I actively do to make some positive contribution, based on my experience?'

There are many examples of people who recover their self-esteem by acknowledging and accepting what they have done as a human failing, forgiving themselves, and then using that knowledge to become stronger and possibly going on to help others.

Positive activity

Think of the number of reformed drug addicts who lecture in schools and colleges, telling their own stories and inspiring young people to better lives; people who have misused alcohol and lecture on the evils of drink – even murderers who go on to reform and live useful lives. Ask yourself, 'If I can't put this right, how can I at least create some good from it?' This might simply mean being open with others about past behaviour and the consequences of it for you, so they have a chance to learn not to take the same path.

Forgiveness

Self-forgiveness is just as important as forgiving others. You need to work on both of these aspects of forgiveness together. How can you forgive yourself if you can't forgive others? Equally, as you learn to forgive others, why can't you learn to forgive yourself as well?

DEVELOPING AS A PERSON TO INCREASE SELF-ESTEEM

Self-acceptance

Self-acceptance is so powerful because it doesn't rely on being good in order to feel good about yourself. Be kind to yourself and strive to do better, to move forward positively – but accept your past imperfections as being normal human frailty, rather than making you a terrible human being. It also means being honest with others about yourself – if you're ashamed to talk about your fallibilities, how can you learn to accept them? There's often the bonus that others don't judge you nearly as harshly as you judge yourself, and you can learn to see things in a different light (see Day 90).

TOP TIP

◆ Don't just dwell on past misdemeanours and let your PFF hound you. Use positive activity, forgiveness and self-acceptance as skills to create or restore your self-esteem.

Change negatives into positives

● If, in yesterday's activity, you could write down – or at least acknowledge – past events for which you feel responsible and leave you feeling guilty and ashamed, now ask yourself the three questions opposite in relation to these events.

● Work on forgiving others for their errors and you'll find it easier to forgive yourself as well.

● Practise self-acceptance (go back and reread Chapter 4 if you need to).

● Focus on others who've overcome troubled pasts by making positive contributions.

● Work out what you can do yourself.

DEVELOPING AS A PERSON TO INCREASE SELF-ESTEEM

> ### Today you will learn ...
>
> what to do when those deep-rooted feelings of worthlessness just won't go away.

In spite of your good efforts, we appreciate that, for some of you, your feelings of worthlessness may be so deep-rooted that nothing you do will shift them.

The ghost of past experiences

Low self-esteem can come from childhood experiences and, where these have been especially traumatic, this is very deep rooted. You've become used to being strongly judgemental of yourself – and this can overspill into being strongly judgemental of others as well. How can you overcome this?

Ways to stop being judgemental

Cold turkey

In the same way that a person who misuses alcohol may need to stop drinking altogether, your own way forward may be to stop judging – completely. You can stop evaluating both yourself and others as being good or bad, right or wrong.

This will require lots of willpower and commitment, but the rewards will be enormous. As you stop judging others, you'll stop judging yourself. You'll come to learn that we can't quantify good or bad, right or wrong. Our views are almost always subjective, and learning to accept them will be really empowering.

Here are some examples of what you could do:

◆ You could give up moral judgements on other people's behaviour. This will be hard – especially in some circumstances – but you could start saying to yourself that they're making what they see as the best choice of behaviour available, according to their own needs and values at the time.

◆ When you read newspapers or watch television news programmes, stop yourself from automatically making an instant 'right or wrong' judgement.

◆ Stop rating both yourself and others as being better or worse than anyone else. Simply accept people as unique individuals.

◆ Stop using critical descriptions, such as 'selfish', 'stupid', 'ugly', 'lazy', etc.

◆ Stop blaming anyone else for your own negative feelings and unhappiness.

◆ Stop judging yourself in any way. This includes your thoughts, your traits and your behaviours. Accept yourself as a fallible human being.

TOP TIP

◆ If you can work on not judging others, you'll be able to be much kinder to yourself. This is an extremely hard skill to learn – you may be amazed that we even suggest it – but we know its huge value in lifting deeply-rooted worthless feelings. So do it!

Activity Practise being non-judgemental

● This is an on-going exercise. On a weekly basis, choose one person you know whom you don't especially like. Consider the specific aspects that you don't like about them (write them down if you need to).

● Now spend some time either re-writing them, or going over them in your mind in a non-judgemental way. Also, if you have contact with this person, practise being pleasant and non-judgemental towards them.

● Be aware of how they treat you in return, and how you feel afterwards.

DEVELOPING AS A PERSON TO INCREASE SELF-ESTEEM

A great deal of the work you've done so far has required you to focus on achieving a specific goal, and then doing what it takes to achieve that goal.

Now, to consistently increase your self-esteem and keep it in good shape, you need to learn to set goals regularly, as part of your life.

Many of you may have heard of the SMART model for goal-setting. If not, the initials stand for: **Specific, Measurable, Achievable, Realistic, Time-limited**

As you make your goal plan today, ensure that each one meets all the above criteria.

What's the most important word in a goal plan? It's action. You can write as much as you like, in as much detail as you like, on as many sheets of paper as you like, but action – doing something – is what will make a difference.

Put your goal plan on paper. Research has shown that when we write down our goals, we have a much, much better chance of achieving them. Your plan should look something like the one on page 234. You might want to adjust it to suit your own needs, but be sure to leave lots of space for very specific ACTION.

> There's no such concept as total failure. There are successes, and there are learning experiences.

Be specific

Make your goals as specific as possible, since that's what makes them easy.

Keep your mini-goals small

Ensure that your goals are *achievable* and *realistic*. We want goals that make it easy for us to feel good and hard for us to feel bad. Ensure they are time-limited too.

Don't overwhelm yourself. Goal-setting needs to become part of your life, not something you give up very quickly because it's time-consuming and leads to more failures than successes.

If one of your goals is to have high self-esteem, you now have a skill and knowledge base to know how to focus on this.

We wish you the richer, better and more confident life you deserve as you achieve success through your efforts. We want you to become pleased to be you!

TOP TIP

- You can achieve whatever you wish if you know exactly and specifically what you want, you have the skills to achieve it – and you have a plan.

Activity

Fill in a goal plan for high self-esteem

Using the tips above, note down your own goal plan for high self-esteem. Consider using similar plans for other areas of your life. You'll achieve more, in less time, and feel good for having done so!

DEVELOPING AS A PERSON TO INCREASE SELF-ESTEEM

225

Refresh your memory

Finally, make sure that you're taking something helpful from this chapter with you. Write down the five most important points you've learned, or now have greater awareness of:

1 ....

2 ....

3 ....

4 ....

5 ....

Instant confidence boosters

- Take dancing lessons.

- Buy a new outfit.

- Think of your three best moments in the last week.

- Find one good trait in everyone you meet.

- Tell yourself you no longer need confidence boosters now that you've finished this book, as you're totally happy with who you are.

- Cheer loudly!

- Remember. You are no longer zero – you are a hero!

Your toolbox is full

You now have 37 skills in your toolbox. It should be pretty heavy by now, and – unless you've got something else you want to add – you now have a full toolkit to use on a regular basis. Don't forget to keep it safely somewhere.

TOOLBOX
Items currently inside
37

APPENDIX A: TABLES

Use these tables as support tools on your journey towards developing self-esteem. You may like to make photocopies of the tables to fill in and keep. If you take the time to complete them as explained in the activities, they will prove an invaluable resource toward increasing your sense of confidence and self-worth.

The emotion you felt	The event that triggered this emotion	What you thought when this happened (self-critical thoughts generated by your PFF)

THOUGHT RECORD (DAY 26)

Date and time, and what happened	What you thought when this happened (How strongly do you believe this? 1–10)	How you felt (How strongly did you feel this? 1–10)	Alternative thoughts (Generate at least 2 or 3 alternatives. Rate your belief in them. 1–10)	How do you feel now? (Rate any possible change, now you've looked at things more positively)

APPENDIX A: TABLES

What happened	What you thought when this happened (How strongly do you believe this? 1–10)	How you felt (How strongly did you feel this? 1–10)	Evidence to support your thoughts	Alternative thoughts (Generate at least 2 or 3 alternatives. Rate your belief in them 1–10)	Evidence to support your thoughts	How do you feel now? (Rate any possible change, now you've looked at things more positively)

Date	What happened/ what did I do? (three events)	What does this say about me that's positive?

APPENDIX A: TABLES

What you have to do	Rate the satisfaction you hope to get from your performance (1–100%)	How much satisfaction did you get? (1–100%) Comment on your rating	Now rate how effectively you think you performed the task (1–100%) Comment on your rating	How do you feel now?

PERSONAL PLAN WEEKLY LOG (DAY 96)

Week 1 (date) ....
Value 1 .... Current rating ....
I have used this value .... times
List the occasions

Improved rating for values 1 ....

Week 2 (date) ....
Value 1 .... Current rating ....
Value 2 .... Current rating ....
I have used these values .... times
List the occasions

Improved rating for values 1 and 2 ....

Week 3 (date) ....
Value 1 .... Current rating ....
Value 2 .... Current rating ....
Value 3 .... Current rating ....
I have used these values .... times
List the occasions

Improved rating for values 1, 2. and 3. ....

Week 4 (date) ....
Value 1 .... Current rating ....
Value 2 .... Current rating ....
Value 3 .... Current rating ....
Value 4 .... Current rating ....

I have used these values .... times
List the occasions

Improved rating for values 1, 2, 3 and 4 ....

GOAL	ACTION I am committed to take time to achieve this goal (must be <u>specific</u>)
On-going (daily)	
Short-term (1 week to 1 month)	
Medium-term (1 month to 1 year)	
Long-term (over 1 year)	

Use your goal plan to work out your needs, and list the action you need to take VERY SPECIFICALLY in order to achieve them. For example, saying "To lose weight" is too vague – how much, by when, and exactly how do you plan to do it?

APPENDIX B: PROFESSIONAL HELP

Where problems of low self-esteem are chronic and deep-rooted, and where you've tried your hardest to eliminate these difficulties on your own without complete success, you might want to consider getting professional help.

Psychological therapy can be extremely helpful in these cases. In this book, we've used what are called 'solution-focused' approaches (cognitive behavioural, rational emotive behaviour and solution-focused practice). If these approaches appeal to you, then you might want to work with this type of therapist or coach.

Insight-based (psychodynamic) therapy will explore your past, looking for unresolved unconscious conflicts that are holding you back in the here and now.

Some therapy is described as integrative, where the therapist will draw on different methods to suit the client and/or the problem at different points in the therapy.

Life-coaching can also be useful where you feel stuck in a rut, as it's a very goal-orientated and motivational approach.

APPENDIX C: ALCOHOL/ABUSIVE RELATIONSHIPS

Low self-esteem as a result of misusing alcohol or abusive relationships can present complex problems. As such, these issues are beyond the remit of this book to deal with in depth, but we want to highlight them and the resources available to anyone who is struggling with these problems.

Low self-esteem and alcohol

For many of us, a drink or two to calm our nerves before a difficult meeting, a daunting social situation, or simply to relax, can be beneficial. But using it as a prop to disguise the real problem – lack of confidence and low self-esteem – can cause people to become alcohol dependent. You may start to make the mistaken connection that you can only cope if you have a drink.

Be brutally honest with yourself about any alcohol dependency. While improving your self-esteem may reduce your reliance on alcohol, be aware that it is addictive. You may find it too difficult to stop on your own.

If you want to reduce your alcohol intake, but would like some help to do so, we'd suggest that you read one of the following books, or contact Alcoholics Anonymous. Don't wait until you have a really serious problem to do this. Nip it in the bud.

Resources

Books

The Thinking Person's Guide to Sobriety by Bert Pluymen (St Martin's Press, 2000) If you're dithering over the 'Do I have a problem?' question, this book will help you decide.

Alan Carr's Easy Way to Control Alcohol by Alan Carr (Arcturus Foulsham, 2002)

Websites

www.alcoholics-anonymous.org.uk
Alcoholics Anonymous official website

www.aamolly.org.uk
For more informal information – an unofficial website full of helpful ideas as well as opportunities to chat via online forums.

Low self-esteem and abusive relationships

Many people – mainly women, but sometimes men as well – stay in relationships that are both verbally abusive and physically violent because their self-esteem is so low that they lack the confidence to leave. These destructive relationships can range from occasional outbursts to regular violence. If you're in an abusive relationship, and wonder if you should leave – or know you should, but lack the confidence to do so – you can get help. Here are some suggested resources (overleaf).

Resources

Books

The Domestic Violence Sourcebook by Dawn Bradley Berry (Contemporary Books, 2001) – includes practical steps for leaving a violent relationship.

Too Good to Leave, Too Bad to Stay. A step-by-step guide to help you decide whether to stay in or get out of your relationship by Mira Kirshenbaum (Maxwell Joseph, 1997)

The Verbally Abusive Relationship: How to recognize it and how to respond by Patricia Evans (Adams Media Corporation, US, 2002)

Website

www.bbc.co.uk/relationships/domesticviolence
Offers support from deciding whether you're really in an abusive relationship to where to go to get help.

USEFUL CONTACTS

Professional bodies and organisations

The following websites provide access to some of the organisations you might want to contact to find a coach or therapist who can help you. Be sure to check that the practitioner is professionally accredited to the organisation that you contact.

Association for Coaching
www.associationforcoaching.com

British Psychological Society
www.bps.org

Association for Rational Emotive Behaviour Therapy
www.arebt.org

British Association for Behavioural and Cognitive Psychotherapies
www.babcp.org.uk

British Association for Counselling and Psychotherapy
www.bacp.co.uk

Association for Professional Executive Coaching and Supervision
www.apecs.org

United Kingdom Association for Solution-Focused Practice
www.ukasfp.co.uk

Centre for Coaching
www.centreforcoaching.com

Centre for Stress Management
www.managingstress.com

United Kingdom Council for Psychotherapy
www.ukcp.org.uk

Contacting the authors

We hope you've enjoyed reading this book and have benefited from the challenging activities. If you want to contact either of the authors directly, their details are as follows:

Professor Stephen Palmer PhD
Centre for Coaching
156 Westcombe Hill
London
SE3 7DH
Email: stephen@managingstress.com

Christine Wilding CMCIPD
Centre for Coaching
156 Westcombe Hill
London
SE3 7DH
Email: chrissyw2@aol.com

BIBLIOGRAPHY

R. Anthony, *Total Self-Confidence* (Berkley, San Diego, 1984)

N. Brandon, *Six Pillars of Self-Esteem* (Bantam, New York, 1994)

M. Bunch, *Creating Confidence* (Kogan Page, London, 1999)

D. Burns, *10 Steps to Great Self-Esteem* (Vermilion, London, 1993)

D. Burns, *The Feeling Good Handbook* (Penguin, New York, 1999)

J. Canfield, M. Hansen and L. Hewitt, *The Power Of Focus* (Vermilion, London, 2000)

A. Carr, *Positive Psychology* (Brunner Routledge, Sussex, 2004)

T. Cash, *The Body Image Workbook* (New Harbinger, Oakland, 1995)

C. Cooper and S. Palmer, *Conquer your Stress* (Chartered Institute of Personnel and Development, London, 2000)

P. Davies, *Increasing Confidence* (Dorling Kindersley, London, 2003)

M. Fennell, *Overcoming Low Self-Esteem* (Constable and Robinson, London, 1999)

D. Franken, *Personal Strengths* (Wellness Publications, Minnesota, 2002)

S. Gawain, *Creative Visualisation* (New World, San Rafael, 1995)

T. Gillen, *Assertiveness* (Chartered Institute of Personnel and Development, London, 1998)

P. Hauck, *How To Be Your Own Best Friend* (Sheldon Press, London, 2002)

T. Laurence, *You Can Change Your Life* (Hodder Mobius, London, 2003)

M. McKay and P. Fanning, *Self-Esteem* (New Harbinger, Oakland, 2003)

C. Padesky and D. Greenberger, *Mind Over Mood* (Guilford, New York, 1995)

S. Palmer, 'Self-acceptance: concept, techniques and interventions' in *The Rational Emotive Behaviour Therapist*, 5, 1, pages 3–30; 1997

S. Palmer, C. Cooper and K. Thomas, *Creating a Balance: Managing Stress* (British Library, London, 2003)

S. Palmer and C. Wilding, *Moody to Mellow* (Hodder Arnold, London, 2006)

M. Perry, *Confidence Booster Workout*, (Hamlyn, London, 2003)

A. Robbins, *Awaken The Giant Within*, (Simon & Schuster, London, 2002)

G. Schiraldi, *The Self-Esteem Workbook* (New Harbinger, Oakland, 2001)

M. Seligman, *Learned Optimism* (Simon & Schuster, New York, 1998)

M. Seligman, *Authentic Happiness* (Nicholas Brealy, London, 2002)

C. Webber, *Get The Self-Esteem Habit* (Hodder & Stoughton, London, 2002)

J. Young, *Reinventing Your Life* (Penguin, New York, 1993)

why not try another title in the

GET A LIFE!

series?

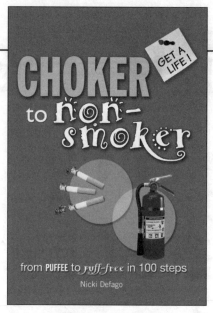

CHOKER to NON-SMOKER
0-340-91540-4

Are you **CHOKING?**
Want to *stop smoking*?
Go from **PUFFEE** to *puff-free* in 100 easy steps!

Top health journalist Nicki Defago will show you how to quit the fags forever and feel great.

How?

Each step of this 100-day program will give you all you need to drop the weed. With 'smoker profiles', interactive quizzes and motivational messages, not only will you give up and stay that way, but you'll also boost your self-esteem. Supporting you at every step, Nicki offers:

❋ Expert psychological tips
❋ Self-assessments and daily activities
❋ Motivational methods
❋ Strategies for success
❋ Exercises and emergency plans

Former BBC journalist **NICKI DEFAGO** has written on almost every aspect of women's health for *Eve*, *She* and *Red*.

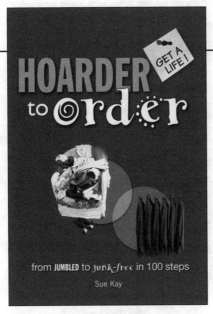

HOARDER to ORDER

0-340-90803-3

Drowning in **JUNK?**
Need to **de-clutter?**
Go from **JUMBLED** to **junk-free** in 100 easy steps!

Decluttering guru Sue Kay is here to help you say goodbye to a muddled head and messy home, and hello to a tranquil and orderly new life!

How?
In just 100 steps you'll go from cluttered to clutter-free, learning habit-changing tips to help you stay this way forever. Don't put it off any longer! Blitz that bedroom and purge that paperwork! This easy-to-follow programme includes:

* Daily activities
* Dos and don'ts
* Action plans
* Self-assessments and quizzes

Professional Organiser and leading UK declutterer, **SUE KAY's** expertise has featured on the BBC, ITV, and in numerous magazines and newspapers.

SKINT to MINT

0-340-90802-5

Are you **FINANCIALLY FLABBY?**
Dreaming of a *money makeover?*
Go from **PAUPER** to *posh* in 100 easy steps!

Finance guru Sarah Modlock is here to give you all the advice needed to refresh your bank account, detox your credit card, and achieve lasting financial fitness.

How?

Your 100-step action plan will give you all the advice you need to transform yourself from penniless to plush. From confronting your cash crisis to sensible spending and even saving for that rainy day, your financial freedom beckons. Each step includes:

* ❋ Daily activities
* ❋ Dos and Don'ts
* ❋ Top tips
* ❋ Action plans
* ❋ Self-assessments and quizzes

You can rely on the expertise of financial journalist **SARAH MODLOCK**, who writes for the major national newspapers and whose articles are featured regularly on Yahoo! and handbag.com.